Beautiful, provocative, tr
ing, and hope-filled, this
single community. Jenily
compelling. She captures the essence of the struggles and blessings of singleness and reminds us that we too can be vulnerable
with God and one another. With grace and humility, she not only
encourages those who are single to live faithfully in God's presence but also exhorts us all to turn to Jesus and to walk with one
another in community. *Singleness: Living Faithfully* is to be read
time and time again by all who desire to know Christ more.
    —**Suzanne R. Bates**, Assistant Professor of Counseling, Cov-
    enant Theological Seminary

Jenilyn Swett has written a Christian account of singleness that is,
first of all, honest about the struggles, challenges, and privileges
of the single life. She grounds her observations in Scripture and
in biblical theology in a way that commends itself for its candor,
its practical wisdom, and its capacity to lead the faithful adult into
both lament and joy.
    —**Daniel M. Doriani**, Professor of Theology and Vice Presi-
    dent, Covenant Theological Seminary

Singleness: Living Faithfully caught me beautifully off guard.
I expected to be encouraged in my singleness with biblical truth
and kindness from a fellow journeyer. This devotional, however,
goes much deeper to provide comforting counsel and practical
exhortation for all of us who are unmarried and desire to live fully
for Christ. I heartily commend this book for anyone who needs
Christ-centered insight on the single life.
    —**Ellen Mary Dykas**, Women's Ministry Coordinator, Harvest
    USA; Author, *Toxic Relationships: Taking Refuge in Christ*

Singleness: Living Faithfully is a richly Christ-centered invitation to
consider the opportunities anda challenges of this unique season
of life in the light of God's Word. With wisdom, compassion, and

biblical insight, Jenilyn Swett guides the reader through relevant questions about gospel identity, relationships, faithfulness, disappointment, and hope. The result is a powerful devotional that is sure to be a blessing not only to single Christians but also to those in the church who seek to love, support, and grow with them.

—**Duke Kwon**, Lead Pastor, Grace Meridian Hill,
Washington, DC

In thirty-one short but thoughtful reflections on singleness, Jenilyn has provided a place for those who are single, married, single again, and married again to reflect on the deeper purposes for our relationships. If you are single, you will find her tone and perspective empathetic, honest, helpful, and redemptive. But if you are not single, please read this as well. It will help you to understand (or remember) the experience of singleness as well as provide wisdom and grace for whatever station of life you find yourself in.

—**Tim S. Lane**, President, Institute for Pastoral Care; President, Tim Lane & Associates; Author, *Unstuck: A Nine-Step Journey to Change That Lasts*

Singleness: Living Faithfully is an incredible resource on a topic often unarticulated. In a compact format, Jenilyn covers a surprising amount of territory with freshly tailored reflections and applications on every page, matching sensitivity with verve and biblical insight with relatability. You will be moved not only to love God and others but also to be loved by God and loved by others. This belongs on every church's bookshelf.

—**S. J. Lim**, Area Coordinator of the Northeast, Reformed University Fellowship

SINGLENESS

31-Day Devotionals for Life

A Series

Deepak Reju
Series Editor

Addictive Habits: Changing for Good, by David R. Dunham
After an Affair: Pursuing Restoration, by Michael Scott Gembola
Anger: Calming Your Heart, by Robert D. Jones
Anxiety: Knowing God's Peace, by Paul Tautges
Assurance: Resting in God's Salvation, by William P. Smith
Chronic Illness: Walking by Faith, by Esther Smith
Contentment: Seeing God's Goodness, by Megan Hill
Doubt: Trusting God's Promises, by Elyse Fitzpatrick
Engagement: Preparing for Marriage, by Mike McKinley
Fearing Others: Putting God First, by Zach Schlegel
Forgiveness: Reflecting God's Mercy, by Hayley Satrom
Grief: Walking with Jesus, by Bob Kellemen
Hope: Living Confidently in God, by John Crotts
Marriage Conflict: Talking as Teammates, by Steve Hoppe
Money: Seeking God's Wisdom, by Jim Newheiser
A Painful Past: Healing and Moving Forward, by Lauren Whitman
Parenting & Disabilities: Abiding in God's Presence,
by Stephanie O. Hubach
Patience: Waiting with Hope, by Megan Hill
Pornography: Fighting for Purity, by Deepak Reju
Singleness: Living Faithfully, by Jenilyn Swett
Toxic Relationships: Taking Refuge in Christ, by Ellen Mary Dykas

SINGLENESS

LIVING
FAITHFULLY

JENILYN SWETT

PUBLISHING
P.O. BOX 817 • PHILLIPSBURG • NEW JERSEY 08865-0817

Library of Congress Cataloging-in-Publication Data

Names: Swett, Jenilyn, author.
Title: Singleness : living faithfully / Jenilyn Swett.
Description: Phillipsburg, New Jersey : P&R Publishing, [2021] | Series: 31-day devotionals for life | Summary: "Singleness is not a problem or a waiting period-it's a unique season of life with its own blessings, challenges, and opportunities. This devotional provides action steps for faithful living"-- Provided by publisher.
Identifiers: LCCN 2021027946 | ISBN 9781629958149 (paperback) | ISBN 9781629958156 (epub)
Subjects: LCSH: Single people--Religious life. | Devotional literature.
Classification: LCC BV4596.S5 S94 2021 | DDC 242/.64--dc23
LC record available at https://lccn.loc.gov/2021027946

For Elise, Avery, Jordan, Samantha,
Isabel, Renee, Norah, and Lily

In memory of my grandmother Charlotte Cecil Swett Walter
and my sweet friend LeeAnn Petty, who both passed away while
I was working on this manuscript. These two beautiful women
lived their respective years of singleness faithfully and showed
me what it looks like to hope and trust in Jesus above all.

Contents

Growing in Maturity

Enduring for the Long Haul

How to Nourish Your Soul

A LITTLE BIT *every day* can do great good for your soul.

I read the Bible to my kids during breakfast. I don't read a lot. Maybe just a few verses. But I work hard to do it every weekday.

My wife and I pray for one of our children, a different child each night, before we go to bed. We usually take just a few minutes. We don't pray lengthy, expansive prayers. But we try to do this most every night.

Although they don't take long, these practices are edifying, hopeful, and effective.

This devotional is just the same. Each entry is short. Just a few tasty morsels of Scripture to nourish your hungry soul. Read it on the subway or the bus on the way to work. Read it with a friend or a spouse every night at dinner. Make it a part of each day for thirty-one days, and it will do you great good.

Why is that?

We start with Scripture. God's Word is powerful. Used by the Holy Spirit, it turns the hearts of kings, brings comfort to the lowly, and gives spiritual sight to the blind. It transforms lives and turns them upside down. We know that the Bible is God's very own words, so we read and study it to know God himself.

Our study of Scripture is practical. Theology should change how we live. It's crucial to connect the Word with your struggles. Often, as you read this devotional, you'll see the word *you* because Jenilyn speaks directly to you, the reader. Each reading contains at least one reflection question and practical suggestion. You'll get much more from this experience if you answer the questions and do the practical exercises. Don't skip them. Do them for the sake of your own soul.

Our study of Scripture is worshipful. As you study your Bible, you will learn God has a lot to say about singleness. There are good days, when your love for Christ is vibrant and truth feels close at hand. There are also hard seasons—filled with loneliness, disappointment, and longing—when your heart feels overrun and singleness feels too hard. But God has not forgotten you. The Father sent Jesus his Son as a testimony of his love and as the great Rescuer to redeem your soul. This gospel plan is the centerpiece of his Word, and he offers it to you. He wants you to know his love. God walks alongside you in your singleness. He opens your eyes to know him better. As we read, study, and pray, and as we meet with believers who teach us about God's riches in Christ, our hope grows. As you grow in your love for the King of the universe, you can't help but worship him. Our study of Scripture leads us to worship.

This devotional provides a wonderful starting point for pondering faithfulness in singleness. If you find this devotional helpful (and I trust that you will!), reread it at a later time to remind yourself about what God and his Word teach us about singleness. If you are hungry for more on this topic, Jenilyn has listed biblically sound resources at the end of this devotional. Buy them and make good use of them.

Are you ready? Let's begin.

Deepak Reju

Introduction

THIS IS NOT the life I expected. I have wanted to be married for as long as I can remember. Growing up, I figured I'd probably marry within a few years after college, have some kids, follow a path similar to the one my parents and many other adults I knew had followed. That is the life that my church, my Christian summer camp, and my college ministry prepared me for. No one ever mentioned the possibility that marriage may not be on the near horizon. Being single was, effectively, just the period of waiting and preparing to find a husband and get married.

I'm nearly forty now. I've had only a couple of significant dating relationships in my lifetime, and I don't know if the Lord has a husband in mind for me, as much as I still hope he does. These years of singleness have not been easy. At times, my singleness has felt like a problem that needs to be solved or even a disease that needs to be cured. At other times, it has simply felt like a holding pattern, as if I am waiting to get married so my life can really begin. Through the years, and through the help of wise mentors, friends, and a lot of prayer, I have come to understand that this is not how God views my singleness.

One conversation several years ago was particularly helpful in reorienting my perspective to align more with God's. I sat with my pastor and shared my disappointment over a dating relationship that had ended before it really even began. My pastor listened and tended to my aching heart, but before our meeting was over, he asked, "Have you ever thought that Paul might have a point?" I asked him to clarify which point he was referring to . . . Paul makes so many, after all.

"About singleness. Paul says that singleness is a good thing. An opportunity to serve the Lord." My pastor was referring to

Paul's commendation of singleness in 1 Corinthians 7, a chapter I always wanted to skip over in my reading: "The unmarried man is anxious about the things of the Lord, how to please the Lord. But the married man is anxious about worldly things, how to please his wife, and his interests are divided. . . . I say this for your own benefit, not to lay any restraint upon you, but to promote good order and to secure your undivided devotion to the Lord" (vv. 32–35).

In contrast to married people, whose interests are divided, single people have an opportunity to focus on an "undivided devotion to the Lord." I don't recall exactly how I responded to my pastor in that conversation, but I'm guessing there was some good-natured grumbling on my part. Nonetheless, his question and Paul's point stuck like pebbles in my shoe, and I was forced to pay attention and continue mulling them over.

Since then, I have sought to view singleness as its own unique season of life, just as marriage is. Each season has its own blessings, its own challenges, and its own opportunities to grow in relationship with the Lord and serve his people. Singleness does allow us to be "anxious about the things of the Lord" (1 Cor. 7:34) in a way that marriage does not, so faithful singleness demands that we ask how we can offer our time, resources, relational capacity, and selves to his service. Singleness also brings particular hardships and burdens, and God ministers in and through those difficulties in particular ways.

As I have spent time talking with other Christians who have been single longer than they would have chosen or expected, or who find themselves single again, I've realized most of us have never been given a clear picture of what faithful singleness looks like. Discipleship in our churches tends to focus on marriage or the path toward it. Many of our ministry leaders, close friends, and family haven't experienced extended singleness themselves. In light of this, we often struggle to find the guidance, support, and sense of community we need to thrive.

If we are to live faithfully in our singleness, we first need to have a solid understanding of our identity in Christ, coupled with a robust theology of singleness. We also need to acknowledge the aspects of singleness that are hard and bring our pain before the Lord. He will be faithful to bring joy and comfort, and one way he will do that is through the love of his people. We need the body of Christ, a local church family, in which we can fully participate as both recipients and stewards of God's grace. These relationships are essential to our growth and flourishing, and, to that end, I hope you'll consider inviting a Christian friend, a mentor, or even a small group to go through this devotional with you.

This devotional is not meant to be a magic pill or Band-Aid. It is meant to offer some insight into how Scripture speaks to the experience of singleness in our culture today. It is also meant to offer some gentle nudges, like the one my pastor gave me, to consider whether Paul might have a point about the benefits of singleness. My hope is that these readings and reflections will be a helpful contribution to a broader conversation about how we can disciple one another when marriage is not a guarantee.

On that note, my voice is just one in this broader conversation. I write as one who has never been married but who still desires marriage. There are single people who don't share that desire or don't feel it strongly. There are others who find themselves single again, whether through divorce or through the death of a spouse. And there are others for whom biblical faithfulness means pursuing a lifelong call to celibacy rather than the same-sex relationships they might desire. For each of us, there are particular ways in which our family dynamics and cultural and religious backgrounds influence our experience of singleness. I hope that even if our personal experiences and longings differ, your time spent engaging with this devotional will still enable you to take encouragement from the truths of Scripture and the invitation to look to Jesus, time and again, in our singleness.

If you are not currently single but are reading this devotional to help you to better care for the single people in your life, I'm glad you're here. I hope this little book will serve as a starting point for conversations and will help you to listen to and learn from the single people you love. You might even consider inviting a single person you know and care about to read and talk through this devotional with you.

This is not the life I expected. But I am abundantly thankful for how God has sustained and provided for me in my singleness, especially through my church family. I have also been deeply encouraged as he has shown me time and again that my singleness, however unwanted, can serve as a blessing to others.

My hope and prayer is that the following pages would be a blessing to you, whatever your experience of singleness has been. As a fellow traveler, I'm glad to have you joining me on this road. More than anything, I pray that the words and ideas here will point you to our Savior and Redeemer—Jesus. He has walked this road before us, he is walking it with us, and he's waiting to welcome us home.

BUILDING ON A SURE FOUNDATION

Before we begin talking about how we can be "anxious about the things of the Lord" in our singleness (1 Cor. 7:34), we need to sink our roots down deep into the Lord himself. Who is he and how has he shown his love for us? What's true about who we are in Christ? God has given us a sure foundation (see Isa. 33:6) on which to build our lives—one that will remain secure throughout every stage of life and every trial. Over the next few days, we'll reflect on several foundational truths.

DAY 1

True Identity

See what kind of love the Father has given to us, that we should be called children of God; and so we are. (1 John 3:1)

IF YOU'VE EVER made a major move, you can appreciate the identity crisis that comes with transitioning to a new place. I felt this keenly when I moved to a different state shortly after my college graduation. It was as if I left my college campus wearing twenty different name tags: roles in which I served, job titles I held, nicknames given by beloved friends—all significant markers of my identity. But a thousand miles away from that community, the name tags were meaningless and were quickly stripped away. It was hard to know who I was and where I fit.

As a single woman in my late thirties, I've had my share of introductory conversations that have involved people asking, "What does your husband do?" or "How many kids do you have?" There's inevitably a bit of awkwardness when they learn that I'm not married and don't have any kids, and the conversation hits a speed bump. My introductory biography on the website of the church where I work always looks a bit thin with no mention of a husband or children. When my married peers find so much of their identity in being spouses and, in many cases, parents, it can once again feel hard to know who I am or where I fit.

In those post-college days, my starting place for rebuilding my sense of identity was the one name tag that wouldn't be stripped away: "Daughter of God." Fifteen years later, that's the name I still cling to, the one that has endured through two more moves, through life changes, and through the ongoing longing to add the name tag "Wife." To be called a daughter of God is an incomparable gift.

John was so deeply secure in his identity in Christ that he referred to himself as "the one whom Jesus loved" (John 20:2). His writings repeatedly speak of God's deep, intimate love for his people as revealed in Jesus (see John 10:14–17, 27–30; 17:20–26; 1 John 4:10–12). It is this love that has been given to us, at such great cost, so that we would no longer be enemies or slaves of God but his *children*. We have access to the creator of the universe because he is our Father (see Rom. 8:14–17). We have a loving advocate in Jesus because he is our big brother (see Heb. 2:17). And we have a secure, unchanging, glorious identity as sons and daughters of God (see Eph. 1:3–14).

This Christian identity is the most important thing about us. We are known and defined, first and foremost, not by our singleness but by our identity as sons and daughters of God. Our marital statuses, addresses, jobs, and church communities may change over time, but our identity in Christ remains constant. Whether we wear the name tags of husband or wife, dad or mom, best friend or housemate, our primary identity will never be found in our earthly relationships. Our heavenly Father looks at us all—single, married, divorced, or widowed—and sees the same thing: his beloved children. And so we are.

Reflect: What are the various "name tags" that you currently wear? Which of these titles, roles, names are most important to you? Which are hard for you to wear? Are there name tags you wish you could be wearing but aren't?

Act: Spend some time meditating on 1 John 3:1 and Romans 8:14–17. What difference does it make in your life to be called a child of God? How does this, or how could it, impact how you think about your singleness?

DAY 2

The God Who Sees

So [Hagar] called the name of the LORD who spoke to her, "You are a God of seeing," for she said, "Truly here I have seen him who looks after me." (Gen. 16:13)

"MISS JENILYN, LOOK at me!" If you've spent any time around children, you've heard an excited plea like this one many times. From the youngest age, we have a deep desire to be seen. We want our joys, our accomplishments, and even our wounds to be noticed and attended to by those who love us.

As we grow up, the longing to be seen persists. At the same time, those who love us often fail to see us, or we look around and realize that no one's watching. This is something I hear often in ministry—a longing for one's toil, pain, worth, and beauty to be seen and validated, as well as the ache that comes when this doesn't happen. Have you felt this ache? Maybe when your contributions at work have been overlooked, or social gatherings are consumed by talk of babies and date nights, or you've endured another long day of single parenting. Of course, enough married people have voiced this longing to be seen that I know marriage is not the cure for this ache, but there remains a sense in which the absence of a spouse can make one feel particularly invisible.

Hagar was a servant and an outsider. She likely spent much of her life feeling unseen—or else seen with disrespect and condemnation. But when she ultimately fled the scornful eye of her mistress Sarai, it was the Lord who chased after her. His messenger found her, called her by name, and spoke words of challenge and encouragement. It was clear from the angel's words that she was seen and known, inside and out. This could have been frightening or caused Hagar to cower in shame, but rather than feeling

19

exposed or condemned, Hagar was drawn to the Lord. His gaze was not cold and critical but caring and compassionate.

That day, Hagar learned that the God of Israel is a God who sees the unseen, those who are vulnerable, those who hide in shame and fear. He not only sees them but also pursues them, listens to them, comforts them, and calls them to faithful obedience.

In our singleness, there are times when we will feel invisible. We will ache for someone to notice our slumped shoulders at the end of a hard day, to affirm good work, to offer a listening ear. But even if we remain unseen by friends or spouses, our God is still the God who sees. He saw Hagar in the wilderness, and he sees you as you work late at your desk, wash another sink full of dishes, let yet another episode play, and shed tears as you try to fall asleep. He sees your dignity, he sees your pain, he sees your toil and calls you to continue in faithful labor under his loving gaze.

Reflect: Do you struggle with feeling unseen? If so, what are the circumstances in which you tend to feel unseen or you particularly long to be seen?

Reflect: Has there been an experience in which you have felt particularly seen by the Lord, as Hagar did that day in the wilderness? How did God remind or assure you that he sees you?

Act: Think of someone in your life who may feel unseen right now. Reach out to this person to remind him or her that he or she *is* seen by both you and the Lord.

DAY 3

The God Who Knows

O Lord, you have searched me and known me! (Ps. 139:1)

PSALM 139 IS a remarkably personal psalm. Reading it feels like eavesdropping on a private conversation between a king and his God. Yet its inclusion in the hymnbook of the Bible means that this is a conversation that we're all invited to have with our God. Throughout the psalm, we're reminded that our God knows our actions, our thoughts, our ways or habits, our words, our physical bodies, our days, our cares and burdens (see also Ps. 94:19), and our sins. Pause for a moment: Isn't it amazing how intimately God knows you?

The knowledge that David describes and praises here isn't the knowledge of a student about a subject or even the relational and physical knowledge of an intimate human relationship. Rather, it is the deep and abiding knowledge that only the One who "knitted [us] together" could have (Ps. 139:13). God knows exactly who we were created to be and what we were designed for (see Eph. 2:10), and he knows how sin has marred our good creation (see Rom. 3:23). He knows our secrets, both those that bring us shame and those that feel too tender to share (see Ps. 44:21).

How can God's knowledge of us as described in Psalm 139 encourage our hearts?

We can be assured that we're never alone, never hidden from his presence. Even in the darkest places, our all-knowing God is still leading us and holding us (see vv. 9–12).

Because God made us and wrote the story of our days, *we can trust that we were created with great care, wisdom, and intentionality.* God's works are wonderful, and that is true of each of us (see v. 14).

When we feel anxious, conflicted, or lost, God knows us better than we know ourselves, and *we can come to him for insight and direction* (see vv. 23–24).

We can be honest with God about our sin. He already knows our "grievous way[s]" better than we do (v. 24), and desires to lead us in *his* way. David knew this very personally: after having his most shameful sins exposed, he received God's forgiveness and ongoing care (see 2 Sam. 11–12; Ps. 51).

We can come to God with our pain, burdens, and deepest longings. We need not minimize our pain or dismiss the ache of our unmet desires. We can find comfort and rest in the fact that even the parts of ourselves that feel most vulnerable are lovingly known. Whether in the darkness and vulnerability of sleep (see v. 18), the womb (see vv. 13–15), or sin and shame (see vv. 11–12), we can follow David's lead by finding reassurance in the Lord's knowledge.

We can rejoice and delight in God's intimate knowledge of us. How wonderful and precious it is that the Lord would care to know us (see vv. 6, 17).

God knows our best and our worst, the beautiful and the ugly, and everything in between. He knows every detail, and yet he loves us still (see Rom. 8:31–39). For me, and perhaps for you too, that is the most wonderful part of all.

Reflect: How do you tend to think about God's intimate knowledge of you? Is it something you welcome, shy away from, or easily forget about? Why do you think you respond to it this way?

Reflect: Which sources of encouragement listed above most resonate with you right now?

Act: Meditate on Psalm 139:23–24. Spend some time praying over these verses, sharing your heart with God and asking him to expose anything unhealthy or sinful in you.

DAY 4

The God Who Promises

His divine power has granted to us all things that pertain to
life and godliness, through the knowledge of him who called
us to his own glory and excellence, by which he has granted to
us his precious and very great promises. (2 Peter 1:3–4)

HAVE YOU EVER heard comments like the following regarding your singleness? "You deserve to be happy!" or "I know God has someone great in mind for you!" or the classic "God will bring you someone when you least expect it!" These words are usually spoken with love and sincere optimism. Do you find yourself tempted to believe such sentiments? Me too. But are they ultimately the most helpful input that our friends and family could offer to us?

Unfortunately, the answer to that question is no. Rather than being founded in the bedrock of God's promises, these platitudes are grounded in the precarious sands of wishful thinking. If we choose to place our hope in sentiments like these, we set ourselves up for disappointment since Scripture never promises earthly happiness or the fulfillment of our desires. We also buy into a distorted understanding of how God works—God doesn't operate according to formulas or hold out on us until we've got everything together.

Peter devoted his life to Jesus (see John 6:66–69), betrayed him, witnessed his crucifixion and resurrection, and experienced firsthand the grace and restoration that Jesus offers (see John 18–21 for the full story). In 1 and 2 Peter, he wrote to churches that were experiencing suffering, "fiery trial[s]" (1 Peter 4:12), and the deception of false teachers. Nice words and sentimentality wouldn't suffice. Instead, he offered Jesus and his "precious and very great promises." Here are just a few of those promises:

23

- Life in this world will be hard, but we will not be left alone (see John 16:33; 14:26–27).
- Jesus intercedes and advocates for us so that we can be in relationship with God (see Heb. 7:25 ; 1 John 2:1).
- As we abide in Christ, the work he's given us to do will bear fruit (see John 15:5–17).
- Jesus is getting ready to welcome us home to a place where our tears will be wiped away (see John 14:1–7; Rev. 21:4).

There's a lot we don't know about how our stories, or the stories of those around us, will unfold. Peter was one of the few who got a preview: Jesus told him that he would be martyred, and Peter still chose to follow Christ. But when Peter asked Jesus how John's story would unfold, Jesus responded, "What is that to you? You follow me!" (John 21:22; see also vv. 18–21).

What do we see in today's verses? Peter knew that his life on earth wouldn't have a fairy-tale ending. Yet he followed Jesus and grew in his knowledge of him so that he could confidently minister to those who faced suffering. Peter assures us that we will be given exactly what we need through our knowledge of the One who has called us to follow him. What a precious and great promise indeed—one that will never disappoint us (see Rom. 5:1–5).

Reflect: What are some platitudes related to your singleness that have been frustrating or harmful to you? How so?

Reflect: In what ways do you look for certainty or hope outside God's promises? What makes doing so easy or attractive?

Act: Drawing from the promises mentioned here or other promises of God, consider how you could graciously respond to one of these platitudes in light of what is and is not promised to you.

DAY 5

Your Body Matters

*Therefore do not let sin reign in your mortal body
so that you obey its evil desires. . . . Offer yourselves to God
as those who have been brought from death to life;
and offer every part of yourself to him as an instrument
of righteousness. (Rom. 6:12–13 NIV)*

I LOVE THAT the Bible tells us that Jesus got hungry. If we
need assurance that Jesus was fully human, we need only look to
this fact. Jesus knows what it is to have a body—to need sleep, to
touch and be touched, to feel the physical impacts of stress and
agony, and to endure the pain of violence.[1] Jesus also knows what
it's like to be celibate in a world of temptation.

This world flaunts and misuses our bodies. Our appearances
are often evaluated on the basis of sexual appeal. Media portrays
those who aren't having sex as prudish or immature. In such an
oversexualized culture, we're also confused about touch—even
the smallest touch or hug can be considered inappropriate or sug-
gestive. This can leave those who are pursuing sexual faithfulness
in singleness questioning our self-worth, starved for touch, and
wondering along with the eunuch if we are nothing more than "a
dry tree" (Isa. 56:3). But Scripture offers a much different message about our bodies.

God chose to reveal his image to the world through embodied humans, and, looking upon his own workmanship, he called
it "very good" (Gen. 1:31; see also vv. 27–30). However, when
Adam and Eve sinned, their bodies bore the consequences. For
the first time, humans would feel shame and insecurity about
their bodies (see Gen. 3:7–8) and pain in their labor (see Gen.
3:16–19). But God left them with a promise: one day the Savior

would come in human form, hunger and all, and claim victory over sin (see Gen. 3:15).

Like Adam and Eve, we bear God's image imperfectly. We sin with our bodies, through our use and misuse of them. Yet, in his letter to the Romans, Paul says through our union with Christ,[2] the only perfect image bearer, we are "dead to sin and alive to God" (6:11) and sin no longer rules our bodies. Now that we "have been brought from death to life," our bodies (and our entire lives) can be instruments of God's work in the world.

In Christ, our very good bodies can labor in our workplaces, homes, and communities. Our bodies can sing and kneel and raise hands in worship; they can move and play and explore God's creation. We can care for one another's bodies through our presence and practical help and by offering loving, respectful touch to our brothers and sisters. And when our very good bodies feel hunger, exhaustion, pain, and even the temptation of sexual desire, we can look to the resurrected body of Jesus. The scars it still bears have secured for us the promise of life more satisfying and beautiful than our culture or any relationship could ever offer (see John 20:24–29).

Reflect: In what ways do you find yourself questioning the goodness or worth of your body? What has contributed to these questions? Consider talking about these questions, or any feelings of guilt and shame you have related to your body, with someone you trust.

Reflect: What are a few ways in which your body has been an instrument for God's work in the world?

Act: Use your body in a purposeful way today—do a physical activity you enjoy, create something, sing or play an instrument, go out of your way to give someone a hug. Thank God for your body and what it can do.

DAY 6

The Gospel Matters

This is how God showed his love among us: He sent his one and
only Son into the world that we might live through him. This is love:
not that we loved God, but that he loved us and sent his Son as
an atoning sacrifice for our sins. (1 John 4:9–10 NIV)

HOW HAVE THE first few days of this devotional hit you? Have
you been encouraged? Has God shown you something new? Or
are you pushing back? Do you wonder whether God really sees
and knows *you*, whether he truly keeps his promises? Perhaps yes-
terday's reading about your body brought feelings of guilt over
how you've misused yours or shame over how others have done so.

Whether today finds you hopeful or hurting, confident or
shaky, encouraged or doubtful in your singleness, let's pause
and ground ourselves in the gospel. Today's passage sums it up:
because he loves us, God sent Jesus to be the sacrifice that would
restore our relationship with him. Why was this sacrifice neces-
sary? Our sin was utterly at odds with God's holiness, our debt far
greater than we could ever pay (see Rom. 6:23). But God himself
paid that debt through the blood of his Son (see Rom. 5:11; Col.
1:19–23), and the resurrection of Jesus brings us from death in
sin to life in him (see 1 Cor. 15:20–28). Why is this such good
news, and why does it matter for our singleness? There are a few
things for you (and me!) to remember.

God loved you first, even when you were unlovable (see Rom
5:8–11). That love remains, and nothing can separate you from
it (see Rom. 8:38–39). When you feel unloved or unlovable, forgotten, alone, or isolated, cling to the sacrificial love of our Father.

If you believe in Jesus, *the debt of your sin has been paid on*
the cross, once and for all (see John 3:16–18; Col. 2:14; Heb.

10:11–14). You can come to Jesus, our "great high priest" (Heb. 4:14) and "advocate with the Father" (1 John 2:1), for forgiveness.

Through Christ's death (not your own efforts), *you are justified*—made right with God (see Rom. 5:18). You're set free from sin's power, and God's work of sanctification begins (see Rom. 6:22–23). This freedom enables you to love and serve the friends, church family, and neighbors God has placed in your life (see Gal. 5:13).

When your singleness leaves you doubting whether God keeps his promises, you can look to the cross and the empty tomb and see that *Jesus's life, death, and resurrection fulfill God's promises* woven throughout the Old Testament (see Gen 3:15; Ps. 22; Isa. 52:13–53:12). God has been faithful, and you can be assured he will keep his promises to you.

Christ's resurrection and our hope of eternal life with him can change the way you experience suffering and the hardships of being single. No matter what comes, *we do not lose heart* because the life of Christ is at work in us (see 2 Cor. 4:7–18).

The gospel is our foundation and future hope. Our response to this good news of God's love is obedient love for him and his children (see 1 John 5:1–3). The remainder of this book will consider what that response might look like in our singleness.

Reflect: Are there sins you need to confess? Bring them to God and remember that those sins have been paid through Jesus's atoning sacrifice.

Act: When is the last time you really meditated on the gospel? Take time today to read through a number of the passages cited here. Invite a friend to read them with you, and discuss how God's Word encourages you today and how you will respond to it. If the gospel is new to you, seek out a mature Christian to talk about it with you.

CULTIVATING

RELATIONSHIPS

In all our various relationships, we are not first and fore-most "single people"—we are children of God (see Gal. 4:5–7). But as sons and daughters of God who are single, we have relational opportunities and relational needs that might look different from those of our married sisters and brothers. I invite you to join me in prayerfully pondering how we can cultivate robust relationships, especially in the church, so that we can pursue faithfulness together.

DAY 7

Belonging to the Body

*For as in one body we have many members, and the members do
not all have the same function, so we, though many, are one body in
Christ, and individually members one of another. (Rom. 12:4–5)*

WHEN YOU THINK of "church," what comes to your mind? A
building? A worship service? A group of people? Scripture offers
a number of metaphors that help us to understand this concept
that is so central to the Christian life, including the description of
the church as "one body" with "many members."[1]

Just as God declared that it was not good for man to be alone
to do the work given him in the garden of Eden (see Gen 2:18),
God's design is that none of us should pursue faith alone. As he
did by providing Eve for Adam, the Lord continues to provide us
with co-laborers for the work he's called us to do. While he does
provide spouses to be intimate co-laborers for some, for all Christians he provides the body of believers. With Christ as their head,
the members of the church work together for God's glory and
their mutual growth (see Col. 1:18; 2:19). Singleness presents
particular challenges and opportunities when it comes to fulfill-
ing our roles as members of the body.

The *challenge* comes in the fact that church can be a lonely
place for single people. Showing up alone, being surrounded by
couples and families, and feeling overlooked by church teaching
and programming can be painful. If we get hurt, it can be easy to
simply withdraw. But as Paul writes in Romans 12, the body of
Christ needs each part, so our absence is a loss to the body.

The *opportunity* comes through a unique interdependence
between single people and the church. We need the church body
to help to sustain us in our pursuit of faithful singleness, and the

31

church body needs us to actively function in the way God has designed us individually. Through this interdependence, we have the opportunity to participate in many of the aspects of long-term relational investment that we long for in singleness: (1) in this spiritual family, we can look to spiritual mothers and fathers, enjoy the fellowship of brothers and sisters, and raise up daughters and sons (see 1 Tim. 5:1–2); (2) we can offer and receive sacrificial love by serving one another, counting others more significant than ourselves, sharing freely of our time and resources (see Rom. 12:9–21; Phil. 2:3–8); and (3) we can exercise and experience fidelity—commitment even when things get tough (see Eph. 4:1–3; Heb. 12:12–14).

In our singleness, we can prioritize and invest in our church family differently than we could if we had a nuclear family to tend to—this is one of our opportunities to be "anxious about the things of the Lord" (1 Cor. 7:32). But we also depend on the body differently than we might if we had a nuclear family to lean on. When we belong to the body of Christ, both our contributions to it and our dependence on it strengthen the body as a whole and bless its members.

Reflect: What has your experience with the body of Christ looked like over time? How have you witnessed and practiced fidelity, self-sacrificial love, and spiritual family in the church context?

Reflect: How has your experience of the church impacted your relationship with Christ?

Act: If your current involvement with the church is not what you want it to be, take a step toward changing that—have a conversation, look for opportunities, begin to pray. If it is what you want, do something to strengthen or encourage the body today.

DAY 8

Tending to Friendships

"Greater love has no one than this, that someone lay down his life for his friends." (John 15:13)

DURING OUR TEENAGE and young adult years, we tend to spend a lot of time with our friends. They laugh with us, cry with us, and often play a significant role in shaping who we become. But as we get into our twenties, work can begin to dominate our time, geographical moves can leave us looking for new friends in new places, and the life stages and experiences of our peers can begin to diversify. With more things competing for our collective time, attention, and affection, and with less opportunity to establish common ground, good friendships can be hard to find and, when we do find them, hard to care for. Later in life, increased work responsibilities, aging parents, and peers who are occupied with children and grandchildren can all be obstacles to friendship. In many stages of life, friendship can easily seem optional rather than essential—a nice extracurricular activity, if you can fit it in.[1]

Yet when Jesus dined with his disciples on the night before his crucifixion, he chose to speak of love in terms of how one loves his or her friends. He told them that the greatest exemplar of love is not one who lays down his life for a family member, a spouse, or even an enemy; rather, it is someone who lays down his life for his friends. That night, as he sat among two men who would soon betray him, and many more who could never love him as much as he loved them, he called them friends (see John 15:15).

This is not the first time that Jesus commended the sacrificial love of friendship. In Mark 2, we see four friends determined to bring a paralyzed man to Jesus so that he might be healed. After his friends carried him some distance, their determined love led them to carry him upstairs and carve out an opening in the roof so that they could lower him down to Jesus. Mark tells us that "when Jesus saw *their* faith" (v. 5), he forgave the man's sins and later healed him. These four friends knew that what their friend needed most was to be carried to Jesus, and in love they did what it took to get him there.

Sometimes we're the friend on the mat. Sometimes we're the ones carrying the mat and digging a hole in the roof. In friendship, we carry one another to Jesus, and, along the way, we show one another the kind of sacrificial love that we can share only because he offered it to us first—laying down his life for us on the cross.

Prioritizing friendships can be a challenge, and friendships can change as a result of time and transitions. The vulnerability of cultivating friendships and entrusting ourselves to others can be risky—Jesus knew this all too well. We will wound others and be wounded in friendship, but even in this, we have the opportunity to practice forgiveness (see Eph. 4:32), to reconcile (see Luke 17:3–4), and to make peace if at all possible (see Rom. 12:18). But whether a friendship lasts for a season or a lifetime, we can love and be loved in a way that reflects the love of our most faithful friend, Jesus.

Reflect: Who have been some of the most important friends in your life? How have you experienced sacrificial love in friendship?

Reflect: What are some obstacles you face to making friends and tending to your friendships?

Act: Reach out to a friend today. Have a phone conversation or make plans to get together, and ask how you can be praying for your friend—carrying him or her to Jesus.

DAY 9

Brothers and Sisters

*Do not rebuke an older man but encourage him as you would
a father, younger men as brothers, older women as mothers,
younger women as sisters, in all purity. (1 Tim. 5:1–2)*

GROWING UP WITH just one sister, I always wanted a brother.
Perhaps it was because I enjoyed my mom's six brothers so much
or because I admired the older brothers of friends. Whatever it
was, I sensed that a brother would add something intangible to
my family that a sister simply couldn't. This is true in our spiritual family as well—God created humans "in his own image . . .
male and female" (Gen. 1:27), so for the church body to function
well together (see 1 Cor. 12:12–27) and bear God's image in the
world, we need men and women serving together.

Of course, life experience tells us that male-female friendships can get complicated, because feelings of attraction can so
easily creep in. Through the influence of both our secular and
Christian cultures, we can view members of the opposite gender
either as potential romantic or sexual partners or as threats. But
Scripture gives us a different lens through which to view the men
and women in our lives: as brothers and sisters.

As sons and daughters of God, through Jesus we have been
made sisters and brothers to one another. Amidst all the aspects
of identity that might change during our lives, this is one that will
remain constant regardless of our ages, vocations, or marital statuses and will last into eternity. Indeed, even husband and wife
are first and foremost brother and sister, a relationship that will
continue even after death ends their marriage (see Matt. 22:30).

In today's verses, Paul exhorted his spiritual son Timothy to
treat the members of his church like family, relating to them with

respect, encouragement, and moral purity. This is one way that Timothy could set an example for believers "in conduct [and] in love" (1 Tim. 4:12), as Paul had encouraged him to do. We can follow Timothy's example by relating to one another like the truest of siblings. What does that look like in your mind?

Within the church family, we have the opportunity to cultivate these spiritual sibling relationships through participating in small groups, serving alongside one another, worshipping together, sharing meals around the family table, and supporting one another in our daily vocations and everyday lives. To name just a few examples, I've seen spiritual brothers and sisters help one another to network for jobs, put a new roof on a friend's house, show up in moments of urgent need (whether related to car trouble, unwelcome rodents, or illness), and enjoy hobbies from kickball to trivia to poetry.

Jesus himself shamelessly calls us brothers and sisters (see Heb. 2:11). I pray that he would help us to follow his lead and to delight in cultivating these sibling relationships within the church. I pray, too, that God would use us in our singleness to set the example for others of how vital and beautiful these relationships can be.

Reflect: How do you tend to relate to members of the opposite gender? Do you find yourself avoiding them, pursuing them, viewing them as potential romantic partners or as threats? Or as siblings? What's led to this?

Reflect: How have you seen the image of God revealed in a particular way by a member of the opposite gender?

Act: Make a point of spending time together with brothers and sisters in your church this week. Enjoy their company, find ways to serve them, and notice how God is at work through those sibling relationships.

DAY 10

Needing One Another

And all who believed were together and had all things in common.
And they were selling their possessions and belongings and
distributing the proceeds to all, as any had need. (Acts 2:44–45)

MY FIRST TIME purchasing household appliances was a glorious team effort. After finding a used washer and dryer online, sisters and brothers from my church helped me to strategize, offered a truck and moving equipment, and showed up to help to get the machines to my place. I barely lifted a finger, and this process was a humbling reminder of my need for others and for the provision of the church body.

In singleness, ordinary needs can bring an added burden because we bear them alone: everything from finding a ride to the airport to being sick to making major life decisions can feel weightier without one consistent person by your side. Do you feel that way? What needs tend to burden you? For some of us, a prideful resolve to be okay on our own can make it particularly hard to voice our needs. But we were never meant to live this life alone (see Gen. 2:18)!

Acts 2 shows us a beautiful picture of what life together in Christ looks like: the church was marked by generously meeting one another's needs. This was part of how these early believers responded to the good news of the gospel, and, in turn, it was part of what made the church stand out to the watching world (see Acts 4:32–37). There's a twofold challenge for us in this.

First, we're challenged to *help to meet the needs of others*. Scripture frequently calls us toward generous financial giving, even if we have only a little to give (see 2 Cor. 8:1–15). As the body of Christ, we are to give of our other resources as well: time, spiritual gifts, creativity, specialized skills. Even small acts of service—delivering a meal or lending a hand with a project—can be ways for us to love one another (see 1 Peter 4:8–11).

Second, we're challenged to *let our needs be known.* How would members of the early church have been able to distribute their resources if they weren't aware of others' needs? For many of us, asking for help can be more difficult than offering it. We don't want to appear "needy" or be "in debt" to others. But what if we truly believed that all the resources among us ultimately belong to the Lord (see 1 Chron. 29:14–16)? What if we took seriously the idea that, in Christ's body, "if one member suffers, all suffer together" (1 Cor. 12:26)? Could we ask for help more readily?

Sometimes we'll ask and be told no. This may be disappointing or discouraging, but we can trust that God will meet our need somehow (see Matt. 6:25–34). Other times we'll get asked to help and need to say no. We all have limits, and it's okay to prayerfully consider what we say yes and no to (see James 5:12). But when the answer is yes, and in a healthy church body it often is, we are blessed with the opportunity to give, receive, and reflect the servant-hearted love of Christ (see John 13:14–15, 35).

Reflect: What makes it difficult for you to voice your own needs?

Reflect: What unique resources do you have to offer in your church body? Is there anything that holds you back from freely offering them?

Act: If you currently have a need, make it known! Talk to a friend or leader in your church. If not, look for an opportunity soon to help to meet someone else's need.

DAY 11

Be Known

And the man and his wife were both naked and
were not ashamed. (Gen. 2:25)

WHILE ADAM AND Eve were still at home in the garden, they
were naked—fully known before God and each other (see Gen.
2:15–25). But the peace and safety of the garden were shattered
by sin and shame. Once they disobeyed God's command, Adam
and Eve immediately covered themselves and hid from God (see
Gen. 3:6–10).

When we're exposed, our first instinct, like Adam and Eve's, is
to feel ashamed. But this was never God's intention for us. We're
meant to feel safe and unashamed when we are known by both
God and others. Yet experience tells us that being known can be a
scary and vulnerable thing, so we often avoid it.

It can be especially easy for single people to avoid being
known. In the intimacy of marriage and parenting, sinful actions
and patterns can oftentimes be more quickly revealed as their
impact causes ripple effects. In singleness it can be easier to man-
age how our sin is seen by others and to hide our sinful patterns.
Do you ever hide your sin from others? What could it look like for
us to let ourselves be known on this side of Eden?

First and foremost, we can let ourselves *be known by God.*
God already knows you more intimately than any human ever
could (see Ps. 139). He loved you, even when you were at your
worst (see Rom. 5:8). We don't have to hide from him, because
in Christ we have nothing to fear: no punishment (see 1 John
4:17–19), no condemnation (see Rom. 8:1), no risk of losing his
love (see Rom. 8:35–39). So rather than hiding in the darkness
and shame of sin, we can walk with God in the light of his truth

and experience God's cleansing and forgiveness through Christ (see 1 John 1:3–9).

Second, we can let ourselves *be known by others*. Walking in the light brings fellowship with God *and* others (see 1 John 1:7). In Christian community, we expose what's hidden in the darkness and bring it into the light (see Eph. 5:8–11) by confessing our sins and inviting others to hold us accountable (see Gal. 6:1–2; Heb. 10:23–25; James 5:16). In the light, we remind one another of what's true and discern together what's "pleasing to the Lord" (Eph. 5:10; see also 4:15).

For most of us, being naked in front of others is the stuff of bad dreams. But God didn't strip the sin-shamed Adam and Eve, nor did he leave them to their flimsy fig leaves. Instead, he graciously made them new clothes (see Gen. 3:21). Now, he's given us an even better garment: Christ himself (see Gal. 3:27), and there is no shame for those who are clothed in Christ (see Rom. 8:31–34).

Single or married, we need fellow Christians who will remind us of this truth. I encourage you to commit to consistently meeting with other Christians one-on-one or in a small group. Doing so can develop the kind of trust and safety that gives us confidence to let ourselves be known as we walk in Christ's light together.

Reflect: What holds you back from letting yourself be known by others and by God?

Reflect: How does knowing that God has clothed you with Christ give you confidence to let yourself be known?

Act: If you don't have other Christians in your life with whom you share the kind of fellowship described here, pray that God would help you to identify one or two people to build that kind of relationship with. If you do, reach out to them today and share something you're dealing with.

LAMENTING
WHAT'S HARD

While Scripture offers us a positive, hopeful view of singleness, that doesn't always reflect our lived experience. In a culture that tends to prioritize pairing up, singleness can be isolating, disappointing, and just plain hard. We don't need to minimize that fact or put a tidy bow on it. Scripture invites us to be honest about our questions, our struggles, our heartaches and to bring them before the Lord. Let's take some time to explore the biblical practice of lament and particular ways we may lament in our singleness.

DAY 12

An Invitation to Lament

*Trust in him at all times, O people; pour out your heart
before him; God is a refuge for us. (Ps. 62:8)*

DO YOU HAVE people in your life to whom you can pour out
your heart? I think of people with whom I know I'm safe; I can
pour out my heart because I feel "at home" with them. In a word,
I *trust* them. I trust their care for me and willingness to listen. I
trust they'll respond with discretion and wisdom. I trust that they
will not love me any less after I've poured my heart out.

How much more can I trust the love of my heavenly Father
(see Rom. 8:38–39) and turn to him, as today's verse invites us
to do? What a gift it is to be able to pour my heart out to the One
who knows me more deeply than anyone and loves me still. This
is the essence of biblical lament: pouring our hearts out to God
and finding refuge in him.

My pastor once described lament as bringing our complaints
to God and talking *to* him about them face-to-face, rather than
grumbling behind his back. It's wrestling with God until we come
to rest in him.[1] The psalms are full of hymns of lament that voice
deep questions to the Lord and speak honestly of external trials
and internal struggles. David shares his sense of God's distance,
the sorrow in his heart, and the threats he faces as he asks, "How
long, O LORD? Will you forget me forever?" (Ps. 13:1). He pleads
for God's help. Yet as he pours his heart out with words that resonate with many of us, he ultimately comes to rest by reminding himself of the character and work of God: "On God rests my
salvation and my glory; my mighty rock, my refuge is God" (Ps.
62:7).

In the garden of Gethsemane, Jesus himself poured his heart

out to our Father, praying in agony that God would spare him from what he knew he was about to face. He lamented not only with his words but with his whole body to the extent that "his sweat became like great drops of blood" (Luke 22:44). Yet the end of his anguished prayers was a surrendered rest in the Father's will (see Matt. 26:36–46; Mark 14:32–42; Luke 22:39–46).

In singleness, there may be much to lament. We'll consider some of these things together over the next few days, and it's important that we do so. Scripture does not ask us to disregard or minimize the suffering of this life. It does invite us to come to the Lord with that suffering, to bring our deepest questions, complaints, and heartaches, and to remind ourselves that we can "trust in him at all times" and find that "God is a refuge for us." Our laments are meant to lead us back to resting in him.

Reflect: Who are some people with whom you've felt safe and "at home"? What about them has made it feel safe for you to trust them?

Reflect: Do you feel the freedom and safety to pour your heart out to God? If so, what enables you to do so? If not, what has been holding you back?

Act: Write a prayer or song of lament modeled on the structure of Psalm 13, another psalm of lament. (1) Cry out to God and bring your complaint. (2) Ask for God's help. (3) Praise God for his character and how he has worked in the past. (4) Conclude with your response to God's work.

DAY 13

Mourning What's Lost

"Blessed are those who mourn, for they shall be comforted." (Matt. 5:4)

As I entered my thirties, I found myself getting sad about aspects of my singleness more often. I grieved when my dad sold my childhood home, in part because I'd never get to bring my (hypothetical) future husband there. I'd drive home in tears from dinners with couples, wishing there hadn't been an empty seat next to me at the table. When I had to make yet another major decision alone, I felt a deep sadness at the absence of a partner. Do you experience grief over aspects of your singleness too?

In Matthew 5, Jesus began one of his best-known sermons with a list of those who would be blessed in particular ways. I'm often hesitant to identify myself with the types of people Jesus describes here—am I meek? Merciful? A peacemaker? Do I qualify for these blessings? I can be especially reluctant to identify myself as a "mourner," especially in relation to my singleness. Many who are single now have endured the loss of a spouse, through either death or divorce, and experience the grief that comes with the ending of such an intimate relationship. But can I mourn something that I've never actually had and that is not promised to me? Is the sense of loss I feel legitimate in God's eyes, even if others might not acknowledge it?

One counselor has studied "ambiguous loss" in singleness: grieving the absence of a person who may or may not exist, without a sense of closure or the ability to move on.[1] Whether or not we're conscious of it, holding out hope for marriage can bring grief with it. A light bulb went on for me when I first learned about ambiguous loss, as it aptly described the sadness I was feeling.

Scripture also affirms this more subtle type of mourning.

Proverbs 13:12 says, "Hope deferred makes the heart sick, but a desire fulfilled is a tree of life." I am grateful that these words are found on the pages of my Bible—they give dignity to my desires by acknowledging the ache that comes when they're not fulfilled. As with any form of grief, there is no quick fix for this heartsickness. Even if you are not hoping for marriage, perhaps you've felt the grief of relational conflict, of letting go of dreams, or of saying goodbye to people or places you've loved.

Jesus didn't specify or qualify the type of mourners who would receive God's comfort—his words apply to all who mourn. The blessing of God's comfort can bolster us whether we are grieving life's biggest losses or smaller, less visible losses. God knows our hearts and knows that continuing to hold out hope can make them sick. He is attentive to our sadness, even catching our tears in his bottle (see Ps. 56:8), and calls us to enter into one another's grief and weep together (see Rom. 12:15).

We'll look later at the unique grief of heartbreak and childlessness and at comfort for those specific experiences, but for all the other aspects of our singleness that we mourn, Jesus offers comfort. We can come to him with our sadness, weary hearts, losses, and disappointed dreams and know that we'll receive the comfort of his presence and compassionate care.

Reflect: What losses or deferred hopes have you experienced in your singleness? What has God's comfort looked like for you as you've mourned?

Reflect: Have you been able to talk about your mourning with others and to bring your lament before God? If not, what's kept you from doing so?

Act: Spend some time journaling or actively reflecting on ways that you are mourning or feeling heartsick right now. Ask for God's comfort, and reach out to talk with a friend too.

DAY 14

Loneliness

Turn to me and be gracious to me, for I am lonely and afflicted. (Ps. 25:16)

I'M FOREVER INDEBTED to a friend who told me that she was lonely in her marriage sometimes. She and her husband were the oldest in our friend group at the time and had been married for about five years. Theirs was a marriage that blessed our community and one that I think we all admired. From my vantage point as a twenty-three-year-old, she had "arrived." But one day I was lamenting to her about the loneliness I felt in being single, and she surprised me by sharing that she could relate. This one conversation reframed my understanding of loneliness. It's not something unique to singleness, nor is it something that would be solved by being in a relationship.

Loneliness is something we all experience on this side of heaven. It's not merely a desire for companionship, nor is it synonymous with being alone. For me, loneliness feels like a restless awareness of a void within me. Something is missing; something is unsatisfied, unfulfilled. At any given time, the empty space may be so small that it's easy to miss or forget about. But at other times, it is so big that it feels like it might swallow me. While it might be easier to notice this void when I am by myself, I have felt it in the presence of others as well. Loneliness tells me that I'm all alone—the only one experiencing what I am experiencing, thinking what I'm thinking, feeling what I'm feeling. No one else could possibly relate, and even if someone could, he or she probably couldn't fill this void.

It can be easy to get stuck in loneliness, but David's lament in today's verse can serve as a lifeline for us in our lonely moments. Can we make his lament our own and admit to God that we're feeling lonely? This takes trust and humility. Can we come to him rather than trying to fill the void we're feeling with lesser things or simply trying to numb our pain? Can we ask for God's attention— for him to turn to us? Can we ask for his grace and pay attention to how he might provide it? Psalm 25 offers some reminders of what that grace looks like: (1) God's truth and guidance, available to us through his Word (see vv. 4–5, 8–10); (2) God's friendship and the invitation to abide in him (see vv. 13–14); and (3) God's salvation, forgiveness, and steadfast love (see vv. 5–7).

Like David, Jesus was well acquainted with the affliction of loneliness. He truly was the only one like himself on this earth (see Heb. 1–2). He was far from home and far from his Father (see John 14:2–4). His earthly friends weren't reliable companions (see Luke 22:54–62). If I am walking the road of loneliness, I can look to the garden of Gethsemane and the cross and know that Jesus has already been down this road (see Matt. 26:30–27:50). As I follow him, I am reminded that this earthly path that can feel so lonely is the path of God's steadfast love and faithfulness (see Ps. 25:5–7), a path that's leading us home.

Reflect: How would you define loneliness or describe your experience of it? How could putting words to your experience help you to lament your loneliness to God and talk about it with others?

Reflect: Have you seen God showing you his grace in the midst of loneliness? How so?

Act: Memorize Psalm 25:16 and let this be your prayer the next time you are feeling lonely.

DAY 15

Rejection and Heartbreak

[The LORD] heals the brokenhearted and
binds up their wounds. (Ps. 147:3)

THOUGH I WISH this weren't the case, it seems inevitable that many of us will experience rejection, unrequited love, or the breakup of a relationship at some point in our journey of singleness. Perhaps we'll experience all three, perhaps repeatedly.

Heartbreak and rejection are messy and painful. Regardless of the circumstances, the ending of a relationship can shake our sense of security and cause us to doubt our worth. Furthermore, many single people deal with not just *particular* rejections (such as an expressed interest not being reciprocated) but a *general* sense of rejection. Months and years that go by without feeling noticed or desired by someone can feel like a constant rejection by no one in particular and everyone in general. And it can hurt.

I've experienced a broken heart more than once and, like David, have experienced unceasing tears (see Ps. 42:3). In times of sadness, today's verse was a precious promise to me, and I clung to the truth that the Lord himself tends to my pain. By God's grace—through his nearness, the compassion of friends, and the gift of time—the tears eventually stopped. Part of my healing process was meditating on how Jesus embodied Psalm 147:3.

- Jesus wept with two grieving women, brokenhearted over the death of their brother (see John 11:35).
- He welcomed those who were rejected by society. Not only did he "bind up their wounds," he also restored their sense of dignity and freed them to reengage with their community (see Mark 5:25–34; Luke 5:12–26).

- When a woman faced the ultimate shame and rejection of being caught in adultery, Jesus shielded her from the punishment of death, advocating for her and offering forgiveness and freedom (see John 8:1–11).
- Seeing his heartbroken mother and beloved disciple, Jesus gave them to each other as he hung dying on the cross. Even in the depths of his agony, Jesus still had eyes to see and a desire to mend shattered hearts (see John 19:26–27).
- To a woman who bore the wounds and shame of numerous broken relationships, Jesus offered his presence, love, and respect. He gave her the hope she'd been thirsting for and the opportunity to introduce many others to the promised Messiah (see John 4:1–30).

When we come to Jesus with our broken hearts, we come to one who intimately knows what rejection feels like, having been rejected by the crowds, his closest friends, and even his Father (see Matt. 26:48–50, 69–75; 27:15–23, 46). He offers healing and hope to our broken hearts through his presence and binds up the wounds of rejection through his forgiveness and restoration. And we need only to glimpse his scars to remind us of how much we are worth to him—no breakup or unrequited love can ever change that.

Reflect: How have you experienced both general and particular rejection? In light of this, what does the fact that Jesus experienced rejection mean to you?

Reflect: Which examples of how Jesus cares for broken hearts particularly stand out to you? What do they mean to you?

Act: Consider the wounds, or scars, you bear from heartbreak and rejection. Pray about them and ask God to show you how Jesus has been at work to bind up your wounds.

DAY 16

Empty Womb and Empty Arms

He gives the barren woman a home, making her the joyous
mother of children. Praise the LORD! (Ps. 113:9)

WAITING FOR MARRIAGE often means waiting for children.
For some, the ache of longing for children may be felt even more
keenly than the ache of longing for a spouse. Have you felt this
yourself or known others who struggle with childlessness? Scripture can seem to rub salt in this wound, proclaiming the goodness
of children and the call of God's people to parent faithfully (see Ps.
127:3–5; Prov. 22:6). But as loud as these proclamations might
seem, we find Scripture quietly honoring two minor characters:
the eunuch and the barren woman. Scripture dignifies the pain of
childlessness by telling their stories and listening to their laments.

A eunuch would have been rendered unable to father children, bringing an end to his family line. In Isaiah 56, the Lord
articulates the eunuch's lament: "Behold, I am a dry tree" (v. 3).
Yet he offers this promise to the eunuchs who embrace his covenant: "I will give them an everlasting name that shall not be cut
off" (v. 5). In God's family, these men would have a legacy.

Scripture tells the stories of many women who were long
childless, including Sarah, Hannah, and Elizabeth. Their barren-
ness brought loneliness, grief, and weary waiting. While these
women's prayers were eventually answered through the birth
of children, children—much like marriage—are not promised
to us. However, the biblical storyline does not leave the barren
woman empty. Today's verse, as well as passages like Isaiah 54,
cast a vision of empty arms one day being filled: "'For the children of the desolate one will be more than the children of her
who is married,' says the LORD" (v. 1).

Although Isaiah's promises for the eunuch and the barren woman will find their greatest fulfillment in the new creation, these promises begin to manifest themselves even now in the family of God. We have the opportunity to serve as spiritual parents to those younger than us in the faith, just as Paul did—addressing Timothy, among others, as "my true child in the faith" (1 Tim. 1:2). Paul did not merely consider himself a mentor, a big brother, or a friend—he considered himself a father in the faith. He modeled this fatherhood for the men in the churches he pastored and called the women of these churches to show motherly care and wisdom (see Titus 2:3–5).

Childlessness—whether in singleness or marriage—can bring deep disappointment, grief, and even shame. Yet even as we wait and pray for a good thing that's not guaranteed, we can look for opportunities to serve as spiritual parents. There are many in our congregations and communities, younger both in age and in the faith, who long to be pursued by spiritual mothers and fathers. Our spiritual children are not consolation prizes—they are part of the blessing we share together in God's family and are a special joy to men and women who long for fruitfulness in their labor to cultivate faith in the next generation.[1]

Reflect: Does the experience of the eunuch, the barren woman, or someone you know who struggles with infertility resonate with you? In what ways?

Reflect: Have spiritual mothers or fathers made a difference in your life? How might they?

Act: If you have a spiritual son or daughter in your life, reach out to him or her today, just to check in. If you don't, look into ways that you might be able to invest in the next generation of young Christians in your church family.

GROWING IN MATURITY

The Christian life is meant to be one of ongoing growth and maturity as God does his sanctifying work in us (see Eph. 4:12–16). Once God has made us his children and united us with the body of Christ, he is constantly shaping us to become more like him—to love the things he loves and to delight in obedience to him (see 2 Cor. 3:17–18; 5:17–21). This is not always easy, but God has promised to equip us for this growth (see 2 Peter 1:3–4). Over the next several days, we'll explore what God's sanctifying work and provision look like in our daily lives as single people.

DAY 17

The School of Sanctification

And I am sure of this, that he who began a good work in you will bring it to completion at the day of Jesus Christ. (Phil. 1:6)

I ONCE HEARD a single man in his midforties reminisce about a church potluck to which the single people in the church were asked to bring potato chips. "Do they think I've survived this long on potato chips? I could certainly bring a casserole!" He shared this to highlight an underlying perception that seems common in our culture: marriage is equated with maturity. Does this sound familiar to you?

Marriage is often described as a "school of sanctification"—a specialized curriculum for Christian maturity. Marriage certainly is an intense means of "iron sharpen[ing] iron" (Prov. 27:17) as husband and wife serve each other, die to themselves, and navigate conflict together (see Eph. 5:22–33; 1 Peter 3:1–7). But this doesn't mean that maturity is a privilege or reward exclusive to marriage. Singleness, too, can be a school of sanctification.

Paul's writings are filled with the language of maturity and transformation, spurring his readers on with the hope of God's ongoing work and an eye toward the glory that lies ahead. Today's verse is offered as a word of assurance and encouragement to the church at Philippi. Paul is confident that when Christ returns, God will complete the sanctifying work that he has started in us. Do you share Paul's confidence about your growth and maturity in Christ? Do you ever wonder, "Lord, how long will I struggle with my particular sins?"

Today's verse also serves as a summary statement, and throughout the rest of this letter we get glimpses of how God carries out his "good work" of sanctification in his people. While Paul is addressing both single and married believers, we can consider particular ways that God is maturing us in our singleness: *God shapes our minds,* enabling us to grow in knowledge and discernment. He strengthens our faith in him and guides us as we follow his will in our relationships and vocations (see Phil. 1:9–10). *God calls us to walk in Christ's humility.* We can seek opportunities to lay down our comforts and freedoms to serve others in our church families and broader communities (see Phil. 2:3). *God redeems our experiences of suffering,* including rejection, loneliness, disappointment, and grief, by bringing us into a more intimate relationship with Christ, who endured all these things and more (see Phil. 3:7–11). *God will enable us to value Christ's righteousness more highly than anything else,* including our own prideful gains and self-sufficiency (see Phil. 3:7–11). *God has made us secure in our belonging to Christ* so that we can press on. With our eyes toward the hope of resurrection, we can move forward even when things seem difficult, discouraging, or hopeless (see Phil. 3:11–16).

The assignments might differ, but God's curriculum for maturity in Christ is the same whether we are single or married. We can join Paul in being sure that God is doing this good work in us and celebrate the evidence of his work in ourselves and others.

Reflect: What are your own perceptions of how both singleness and marriage relate to maturity? How have these developed? Do they reflect a biblical view of Christian maturity?

Reflect: How has God's good work of sanctification been happening in your life lately?

Act: Consider something you could do today or this week to serve someone in a way that goes beyond what is expected or convenient. In other words, don't just bring potato chips to the meal—bring a casserole and offer to help with dishes afterward!

DAY 18

Waiting Well

*"The LORD is my portion," says my soul, "therefore I will
hope in him." The LORD is good to those who wait for
him, to the soul who seeks him. (Lam. 3:24–25)*

ONE WINTER EVENING, I joined a family I love for dinner,
and the kids were promised that their meal would be followed
by a trip to McDonald's for ice cream. The family had recently
acquired a karaoke microphone, and in the course of cleaning up
after dinner, a round of karaoke got started. Before long, three
adults and two kids were dancing, laughing, and singing our
hearts out. But a third kid slumped on the sofa, pouting, because
all she wanted to do was go get her ice cream.

It hurt my heart to watch her miss out on so much fun because
she couldn't stop thinking about that ice cream. Her brother and
sister were waiting for ice cream, too, but they were able to enjoy
the wait. She was purely miserable.

I recognize myself in her. Do you struggle with waiting too?
In my singleness, I can focus so much on the thing I'm waiting
for that I can't see what God is doing right now. I act as if things
are on hold until a husband comes on the scene or some other
dream is fulfilled, and that holding pattern often involves squan-
dered time and misery. So what does it look like for me to pick
up the microphone and sing my heart out rather than pout as I
wait?

First, I must remember that all God's people are waiting for
something. Countless stories and refrains in Scripture remind us
that we are waiting for healing and justice (see Isa. 61), for restoration (see Rom. 8:18–25), for Jesus to come and make all things
new (see Rev. 21:1–7). And in the day-to-day, we're waiting for

news to come, a job to change, school to be over, relationships to be mended. We are a waiting people. I am not alone in this.

But second, I must remember that what matters most is the *object* of my waiting. It can't be the temporary things of this world. My hope is not ultimately in marriage, children, buying a house, getting a promotion, or my next vacation. My hope is in the Lord, and I must examine whether or not I am seeking him above all else. Today's verses from Lamentations serve as a bedrock reminder that our good God is providing for and working on behalf of those who are waiting for him, even when the waiting feels long and hard.

The author of Lamentations longed for justice, restoration, and deliverance, but ultimately he longed for God. The Lord doesn't promise that our waiting time will be all singing and laughter, but he does promise himself. So we can look for and trust his presence in our waiting. As we seek him, we can see more clearly how he would have us use our waiting time.

Reflect: What are you waiting for right now? In what ways are you waiting on the Lord rather than just waiting on a change in your circumstances?

Reflect: Consider a time when you have experienced God's goodness in the midst of waiting. How did this sustain you in your waiting? What did this reveal to you about who God is?

Act: Think about something good and redemptive you've been putting off doing until your circumstances change. Take steps to do that thing, or something like it, this month. Get creative, grab a friend or two to join you, and enjoy this experience as a reminder of God's goodness, even in our waiting.

DAY 19

Fear and Anxiety

*"Therefore I tell you, do not be anxious about your life, what
you will eat or what you will drink, nor about your body,
what you will put on. . . . Which of you by being anxious can
add a single hour to his span of life?" (Matt. 6:25, 27)*

FEAR, ANXIETY, AND worry are familiar to most of us. We
worry about finances and job security. We fear sickness, death,
and loss. Sometimes our worries are like white noise, barely
noticeable in the background. At other times, our anxieties might
become distracting, impacting us physically, mentally, and rela-
tionally. In some cases, our fears can be paralyzing, keeping us
isolated and preventing us from functioning day to day or moving
forward.[1]

Singleness can bring up fears and anxieties that those who are
married may not experience (and vice versa). Who will care for
me if I get sick or lose my job? How will I navigate major decisions or life transitions alone? What if I never get to experience
the physical intimacy of marriage or never have the opportunity
to have kids? Who will visit me in the nursing home when I am
elderly? Who will plan my funeral? One worry leads to another,
and we can quickly spiral into despair.

In Matthew 6, as Jesus spoke to a crowd of people who had
anxieties of their own, he addressed their worries. He called their
attention to their heavenly Father who cares for them: "Look!
Look at the birds flying overhead. Look at how God feeds them!
Admire those lilies over there. Run your hands through the grass
and see how God clothes them! The One who cares for these cares
even more for all of you!" (see vv. 26–30). It's an argument from
the lesser to the greater: If God cares for the birds and the lilies,

how much more will he care for you? When we set our eyes on our heavenly Father, faithfully seek after his kingdom rather than seeking own comfort and security (see v. 33), and notice the evidence of his providential care, our fears are put into perspective.

Jesus said we will have trouble in this world (see John 16:33). Our worst fears might come to pass. We may face circumstances we haven't even imagined needing to fear. But in today's passage, he tells us to take trouble one day at a time rather than preoccupying ourselves with needless worry about trouble that may lie ahead (see Matt. 6:34). God knows the needs we have day by day, and he gives us what we need for "life and godliness" (2 Peter 1:3; see also Matt. 6:11).

Lifting our eyes from our worries and looking up to our Father also gives us the chance to see that we're not alone. Our fears can so easily isolate us, but when we raise our eyes and look around, we find ourselves surrounded by brothers and sisters. As we grapple with our fears together, we can help each other to seek his kingdom and call one another's attention to both big and small reminders of God's care.

Reflect: Look back on a situation in your life that was difficult or scary. How can you see God's provision for you in and through that situation?

Reflect: What are some fears or anxieties you have that specifically relate to singleness? Have you shared these with anyone else? If not, who could you share them with?

Act: With those fears and worries in mind, do something that will help you to pay attention to God's work in creation—take a walk, buy a bouquet of flowers, watch a nature documentary. If you can, do this with a trusted Christian friend. Consider together how God's handiwork can encourage you to trust his provision in each day's trouble.

DAY 20

Preaching to Our Self-Pity

But this I call to mind, and therefore I have hope . . . (Lam. 3:21)

DOES THIS THOUGHT process sound familiar to you? It starts in a moment of disappointment, loneliness, or feeling excluded. The lies and the woes start to come one after another: I am unseen, unwanted, forgotten. I feel angry and disappointed with everyone in my life. Before long, I've convinced myself that no one, not even God, cares about me and that I'll be alone forever.

This spiral of self-pity is one that I've seen many go down, but I recognize it only because I've been stuck in it so many times myself. Self-pity can be defined as "a self-indulgent dwelling on one's own sorrows."[1] When we allow ourselves to be consumed by it, to dwell in sorrow and insecurity, we forget that we already have a secure dwelling place in God (see Ps. 91) and that Christ himself dwells in us (see Eph. 3:14–19). We get stuck in sinful unbelief, failing to take hold of the sure hope we have in the gospel (see Heb. 6:13–20). We get so self-focused that we're likely to sin against others in our judgmental thoughts toward them.

Self-pity can be particularly tempting for single people. It seems to thrive in isolation, and extended time alone can be fertile ground for it to grow. Anecdotally, it also seems that being a numerical minority—as many single people are in their churches and social circles—can contribute to this feeling. Knowing this, we must be prepared to fight against self-pity, especially since it only serves to further distance us from God and one another. Have you ever wrestled with self-pity? If so, what does it look like in your life?

In Lamentations 3, the author recounts the afflictions he's seen and experienced, placing the blame on God for all that he's endured. He himself seems to be going down this self-pity spiral, concluding that he is without peace, has lost all hope, and doesn't even remember what happiness is (see vv. 17–18)! However, he doesn't let himself get stuck in that hopeless place. With a pivotal "But . . ." he begins his climb back up by preaching to himself, interrupting his spiraling thoughts to remind himself of what's actually true. This provides a model for when we need to do the same. Based on verses 22–26, we can call to mind God's *character* (he is loving, faithful, and good); his *steadfastness* (he is constant and does not change); his *mercies* (he provides daily for us); and his *salvation* (he offers us forgiveness and grace in Jesus).

When we find ourselves joining the author of Lamentations in recounting our afflictions, we can follow his lead and preach the gospel to ourselves. Our hope is in the Lord—not in ourselves, others, a change in our circumstances, or the end of our afflictions but in the One who has been faithful and steadfast throughout generations. As we dwell in him, we can freely repent of our sins against God and others, bring our sorrows and burdens to Jesus (see Matt. 11:28–30), and celebrate how God's mercies bring hope each day.

Reflect: What tends to send you down the self-pity spiral or prompts you to start recounting your afflictions? If you're not sure, talk about this with a friend or counselor.

Reflect: In what ways does self-pity distance you from God and others?

Act: Read Lamentations 3:1–26. Talk about this passage with a trusted friend or mentor. What is something you could do now to make it easier for you to call these truths to mind the next time you're stuck in self-pity? How could your friend hold you accountable to this?

DAY 21

Practicing Hospitality

Welcome one another as Christ has welcomed
you, for the glory of God. (Rom. 15:7)

WHAT IS YOUR initial reaction to today's topic? Does the word *hospitality* make you cringe? Tune out? Say, "This is for someone else, not for me!"? Or are you eager to fire up the grill or put on the kettle and invite someone over? Whatever your reaction, as followers of Jesus, we are all encouraged to practice hospitality— but perhaps you and I are defining the word a little differently.

Hospitality is about welcoming others into a space where needs are met and comfort is offered; in other words, it's about making people feel at home, in the broadest sense. This can certainly happen in your home (however big or small), but it can also happen in a coffee shop, in the office break room, at your Sunday morning pew, and even over a phone call.

In Romans 15, Paul calls readers to extend the same welcome we've received in Christ. In verse 3, he reminds his readers that "Christ did not please himself" but worked for the good of others. Jesus laid down his life so that we could be welcomed into the family of God, the consummate host. From the very beginning, in Eden, God created a home where all our needs could be met, including our need for the constant comfort of his presence (Gen. 3:8). Even when Adam and Eve's sin resulted in their being exiled from this perfect home, God continued to provide for their needs, making garments for them and leaving them with hope that this was not the end of the story (see Gen. 3:14–15, 20–21).

Since the day Adam and Eve left Eden, humans have been homesick. But God has constantly urged his people to offer glimpses of home by extending hospitality to others—sojourners, strangers, orphans, and fellow believers (see Deut. 24:19–22; Heb. 13:2; 1 Peter 4:9). Hospitality is not about entertaining, or impressing others, or making ourselves look good. Rather, it's about seeking the good of others and giving them a tangible experience of Christ's welcome. We can do this in any and every stage of life. I've seen single people practice hospitality by

- sharing meals, whether by delivering dinner (take-out or homemade) to friends or pushing through their insecurities and inviting others over for dinner or dessert;
- keeping toys on hand for times when kids come over;
- coordinating gatherings to celebrate holidays and meaningful events in others' lives;
- making church a welcoming place for others by volunteering to make the coffee or serve as a greeter or by initiating lunch outings after church with a variety of people; and
- creating an inviting office space—including a stash of snacks!

No matter how much or how little we have, how confident we feel, or what our personalities are like, we all have some God-given capacity to make time and space for others and invite them into conversation and meaningful connection. This is how we respond to and reflect the welcoming heart of Jesus.

Reflect: How have you experienced the welcome of Christ in your life? How have others reflected his heart of welcome to you?

Reflect: What excites you about practicing hospitality? What keeps you from doing it?

Act: Think of one opportunity you have, or could create, this week for making space and time to welcome someone and help that person to feel at home. Pray about it, and make it happen!

DAY 22

Sabbath Rest in Singleness

"Remember the Sabbath day, to keep it holy. Six days you shall labor, and do all your work, but the seventh day is a Sabbath to the LORD *your God. On it you shall not do any work." (Ex. 20:8–10)*

COUNTLESS THINGS COMPETE against God's command for us to keep the Sabbath day, especially in our 24-7 world. As single adults, we may face temptations to work nonstop or encounter obstacles to maintaining a healthy rhythm of work and rest. Without kids to pick up from school or spouses awaiting our arrival at home, it can be easy to stay late and pick up the slack at the office or to fill our evenings with activities. Our weekends get spent on life-maintenance tasks, like running errands or paying bills. It can be tempting to stay in bed and catch up on sleep on Sunday morning rather than getting up for church.

The command to honor the Sabbath reminds us that our time belongs to God, and he wants his people to devote time to him just as we would devote time to anyone we love. It is also proof that God did not create us to labor nonstop. Indeed, we were created in his image, and even he rested after his labors of creation (see Gen. 2:2–3). Just as he set apart that seventh day, the people of Israel were commanded to set apart a day for rest and worship. As we continue to follow God's design for a weekly rhythm of work, rest, and corporate worship, we have the opportunity to honor our Creator, humbly acknowledge our limits, and seek refreshment in fellowship with God and others.

God's Sabbath command requires a response from us. How can we function within our God-given limits and protect time for restorative worship, rest, and fellowship? Here are a few suggestions:

- Unless your work schedule prohibits it, guard Sunday as a day of worship, rest, and fellowship with God's people (see Heb. 10:25). Get work tasks, household chores, and errands done throughout the other six days of the week. If you need a sleep-in day, make it Saturday, and look forward to a restful Sunday afternoon nap after church.
- In addition to participating in worship on Sunday, be intentional about spending time with your church family, whether that's attending a small group in the evening, sharing a meal, or meeting up to toss a Frisbee and enjoy God's creation together.
- Regularly devote time to being in solitude with God—reading your Bible, praying, journaling, reading books that draw you closer to him. Even Jesus needed this kind of time with God (see Mark 1:35).

The Sabbath is meant to be not a burden but a benefit to us (see Mark 2:27). This weekly rhythm of rest with God and his people nourishes us for the six days ahead and reminds us that we worship a God who never sleeps and who makes things grow while we do (see Ps. 121:4; 1 Cor. 3:6).

Reflect: What aspect of the Sabbath presents the biggest challenge for you: participating in corporate worship, resting from work, engaging in solitude with God, or fellowshipping with your church family? What makes this a challenge?

Reflect: What is the difference between *relaxing* and *resting with God*? How can you best experience rest with God?

Act: Look at your schedule and plans for the next week. Commit to making one change that would enable you to more freely honor and enjoy the Sabbath. Tell a friend or mentor about your commitment so he or she can hold you accountable.

DAY 23

Discernment in Dating

It is my prayer that your love may abound more and more, with knowledge and all discernment, so that you may approve what is excellent, and so be pure and blameless for the day of Christ. (Phil. 1:9–10)

DATING: FUN? HOPEFULLY. Scary? Maybe. Complicated? Probably. Confusing? Definitely. How do you feel when this topic comes up? Dating may not be a part of every single person's experience, but chances are good that someone in your life will encounter the complicated confusion of dating. What guidance does Scripture offer us in this area?

For modern dating and the many other aspects of life the Bible doesn't explicitly address, God has given us the Holy Spirit, the whole counsel of Scripture, and discernment. In Philippians 1, Paul prays for increasing discernment—a growing love and knowledge of Jesus that informs our understanding of what he'd consider "excellent," which is exactly the kind of insight we need for dating.

First, we must be discerning in *how* we date. It's important to seek God's guidance and talk with trusted mentors and friends about how to approach dating in a way that is healthy and faithful (see Prov. 27:17; Phil. 4:9). This might look a little different for each person depending on his or her story and context.

Second, we must be discerning in *who* we date. Dating apps sell us the chance to find the person who's most available or to hunt for the "perfect" match. These approaches can be attractive but can lead to all sorts of problems and unrealistic expectations. It's important to remember that no matter who you date, he or she will be a sinful human just like you, but hopefully you'll see in this person the ongoing transformative work of Christ's grace (see 2 Cor. 3:18) and the fruit of the Spirit (see Gal. 5:22–23).[1] No matter what, you are brother and sister in Christ, and this person is worthy of respect, dignity, and loving care.

Third, we must exercise discernment *while* we date. Dating reveals things about what we value and prioritize, how we've been raised, how we function in a relationship, what God is calling us to individually and (perhaps) together. Is this a relationship that's moving toward becoming a godly marriage (see Eph. 5:22–33)? This discernment can't happen in a vacuum. We need input from our community—from people who know and love us and who will ask us good questions, hold us accountable, offer their perspective, and be there no matter what the future holds.

Dating can be a risky thing, and many of us have been lovingly cautioned to "guard our hearts."[2] While we certainly don't want to be reckless with our hearts, the reality is that opening ourselves up to *any* relationship requires some risk. To take that risk, we must remember that ultimately God is the one who guards our hearts (see Phil. 4:7). With our hearts safe in him and with guidance from our church family, we can embrace dating as an opportunity to learn more about ourselves, a sibling in Christ, and God's will (see Rom. 12:2). Whether or not dating leads to marriage, practicing discernment will keep us "pure and blameless" for the day when Jesus calls us home.

Reflect: How do you tend to approach dating? What do you think the goal of a dating relationship is?

Reflect: How has dating (or not dating) influenced your view of yourself and your relationship with God?

Act: Talk about it! Talk to a trusted friend, a ministry leader, or your small group. Share what's on your mind when it comes to dating, and talk about how your community can walk with you.

DAY 24

Sexual Faithfulness

Flee from sexual immorality.... Do you not know that your
body is a temple of the Holy Spirit within you, whom you have
from God? You are not your own, for you were bought with a
price. So glorify God in your body. (1 Cor. 6:18–20)

MANY OF US who grew up in church learned one primary thing about sex: we should save it for marriage. And while never stated outright, there was an implicit assumption that we'd all get married in our early twenties. There wasn't much talk about what to do with our sexual desires until then, and there was absolutely no discussion about the potential of remaining single.[1] So now we've got to ask: What does sexual faithfulness[2] look like when we're single?

The Bible makes it clear that God created sex to be a good thing—a physical expression of the intimate union of marriage and the means through which new life is conceived (see Gen. 1:28; 2:23–25). But sex can also be powerfully destructive, and the sexual union of marriage is meant to be honored and protected (see Ex. 20:14).

Sexual immorality was especially rampant in the culture of Corinth when Paul was writing. He pleaded with the Corinthian church to "flee from sexual immorality." Since Paul commends sex within marriage (see 1 Cor. 7:1–5), we know he didn't do this because he was a prude or a curmudgeon. He made this plea because our bodies are not our own; we are members of Christ's body (see 1 Cor. 6:15), we belong to Christ because we were purchased with his blood, and our bodies are the place where God's Spirit dwells. Therefore, Paul's conclusion is that we are to glorify God by being good stewards of our bodies, which means pursuing sexual faithfulness rather than sexual immorality (see 1 Cor. 6:13).

The world offers us many temptations: pornography, masturbation, "casual" sex, sex in dating relationships, and the like. But faithfulness to God's design for sex, our bodies, and our relationships means *fleeing* sexual immorality—running in the opposite direction and avoiding it at all costs.

What does this look like, practically? It looks like studying God's view of sex through Scripture and helpful resources that explain a biblical theology of sexuality.[3] It looks like praying for and practicing self-control (see Gal. 5:23; 2 Tim. 1:7). Through the Holy Spirit, God's given us the means to resist temptation (see 1 Cor. 10:13), delay gratification (see Rom. 13:14), and endure the pain that doing so sometimes entails. It looks like avoiding situations or media that might present undue temptation (see Matt. 5:27–30). It looks like examining whether there are physical, emotional, relational, or spiritual needs underlying our sexual desires. There may be God-honoring ways for those needs to be met, or we may need to offer our unfulfilled sexual desires as a living sacrifice to the Lord (we'll look at that on day 27). And it looks like repenting of past sexual sins, seeking Christ's forgiveness, and knowing that in Christ we are free (see Ps. 103:12; Mal. 3:7; Rev. 1:5; 3:19).

As we looked at on day 5, God created our bodies, and they are very good (see Gen. 1:27–31). Fleeing sexual sin and pursuing sexual faithfulness is just one way we can offer our bodies to God as instruments for righteousness (see Rom. 6:13) and glorify him.

Reflect: What have you been taught—both explicitly and implicitly—about a biblical view of sex and sexuality?

Reflect: What does it mean to you that "you are not your own, for you were bought with a price"?

Act: Choose one of the practical ideas above to focus on as a next step. Spend some time praying or journaling, talk with a friend, or seek guidance from a trusted ministry leader.

DAY 25

The Discipline of Rejoicing

Rejoice with those who rejoice, weep with those who weep. (Rom. 12:15)

IN ROMANS 12, Paul begins to apply the gospel to the daily lives and interactions of the Christian community. In verse 15, he exhorts its members to empathize with one another—to share in the emotional experiences of grief and joy. All the things that Paul calls Christians to in verses 9–21—love, patience, eager service, generosity, humility—can be challenging or costly, so it used to seem strange to me that Paul would have to command us to rejoice with others too. Isn't this a no-brainer? But over time, and especially as my own singleness has persisted, I've been surprised to discover just how difficult it can be to "rejoice with those who rejoice."

When another engagement is announced on social media, sometimes envy comes more quickly than joy. When wedding invitations and birth announcements bombard one's mailbox, bitterness or resentment well up, rather than rejoicing. And when yet another dear friend faces a major life transition and you feel left behind, it's hard to smile with happiness when you're fighting back tears of grief.

Have you struggled to rejoice with someone who's rejoicing? The ability to rejoice with another person comes through the work of the Holy Spirit and our own faithful pursuit of growth in grace. When rejoicing doesn't come easily, what can we do?

Pray. If God has asked something of us, he will give us what we need to accomplish it (see 2 Peter 1:3–4). Ask for the Holy Spirit's help to rejoice.

Participate. We rejoice together in the body because one member's joy is another's (see 1 Cor. 12:26). Find cause for your own joy in the midst of another's—perhaps it's looking forward to a great party on the wedding dance floor, picking out beloved children's books to give as a baby gift, or treating a friend to dinner at a favorite spot to celebrate a promotion.

Practice the discipline of rejoicing. Seek out meaningful ways to acknowledge a friend's cause for joy. That might mean sending a card or text, buying a gift or attending a celebration, or simply listening as a friend shares his or her excitement.

Ponder. Examine your heart—is there a root of bitterness growing there? Is there envy or covetousness?

Pour out your heart. If your pondering has led to conviction, bring your confession to God. If another person's joy is cause for your weeping, take time to express your lament both to God and to a trusted brother or sister who can weep with you.

One young man longed to be married. He watched his roommate, a close friend who hadn't felt a strong desire for marriage, date a young woman who had all the characteristics he himself would have looked for in a wife. The pain of witnessing this growing relationship while feeling the disappointment of his own unmet desires was so great he considered moving out. But he sought the Lord and prayed for a heart that could rejoice with his friend, and over time the Holy Spirit enabled him to rejoice. Rejoicing with others can be costly, but it is evidence of the Spirit's sanctifying work in our hearts.

Reflect: Does rejoicing with others come naturally to you? If not, how do you tend to react when others are rejoicing?

Reflect: How could rejoicing with others be an act of sacrificial love?

Act: Whether it's easy or difficult, take time to practice the discipline of rejoicing with someone this week—celebrate with him or her whether over a birthday, an accomplishment, or a life transition.

DAY 26

Honoring Marriages

Let marriage be held in honor among all, and let the
marriage bed be undefiled. (Heb. 13:4)

I WAS ONCE asked to hold on to a couple's wedding rings in the hours before their wedding. I was struck by the weightiness of this task, not only because of the monetary value of the pieces I held but because of the significance of what they represented: my friends' covenant commitment to one another. The truth is that, in community, we all share responsibility for helping our friends to uphold their marriage covenants.

The author of Hebrews writes to believers to remind them of their dependence on one another in the race of faithful endurance. Hebrews 13 begins, "Let brotherly love continue," and the writer expands on what that entails: practicing hospitality (see v. 2), caring for the imprisoned and mistreated (see v. 3), and seeking contentment rather than greed (see v. 5)—as well as honoring marriage. It's the responsibility of the whole church community—married *and* single—to honor the marriages in its midst.

A marriage needs the brotherly love of the community to flourish. Husband and wife need friends who won't merely listen to their complaints about each other but point them back to their marriage vows. One single friend did this for a couple impacted by a betrayal in their marriage. She tirelessly came alongside the wife to listen to her, encourage her, challenge her, and help her to get the care she needed to keep fighting for her marriage as her husband did the same. That wife now says, "She was our relationship's greatest champion. Without her, we would not be married."

How might God use you to champion a friend's marriage? We can pray for our friends' marriages, encourage them to keep connecting with each other, and simply enjoy sharing life with them. We can also be friends who help to shoulder their burdens and share their joys individually, since no spouse is meant to be everything to his or her partner.

Brotherly love means "[letting] the marriage bed be undefiled" as well. This is certainly a call to marital fidelity, but in a passage that's focused on the community, this means that the whole church is responsible for pursuing sexual integrity and honoring the marriage covenant. This means exercising wisdom in setting and respecting boundaries, but it also means creating safe places to talk about sexual struggles and sin. It means helping married couples to discern what a healthy, God-honoring sexual relationship looks like for them.

We may not be involved in the intimate details of these conversations, but we can point our married brothers and sisters toward the discipleship and support they need.[1] Sharing honestly about our own sexual struggles may also open up dialogue for others. For instance, when I first started sharing publicly about my struggles with masturbation, many married women admitted that it was an ongoing struggle for them too. Talking with them about this was a way of holding their marriages in honor.

Honoring and upholding the marriages in our midst may demand sacrifice from us. But as brotherly love continues, we may also find that we are deeply blessed by the flourishing marriages around us.

Reflect: Who are some married couples in your life? How have you had opportunity to honor their marriages?

Reflect: How has your singleness held you back from befriending or actively supporting married couples?

Act: Reach out to a married friend and ask how you can be praying for his or her marriage this week.

DAY 27

A Living Sacrifice

I appeal to you therefore, brothers, by the mercies of God, to
present your bodies as a living sacrifice, holy and acceptable
to God, which is your spiritual worship. (Rom. 12:1)

I ONCE SAT across from my counselor lamenting (or possibly whining about) the difficulty of obeying God's commands. I was particularly thinking of what I was missing out on or giving up by pursuing sexual faithfulness and committing to date only fellow believers. The pain of obedience seemed pointless and unfair—did it even matter to God? My counselor asked, "What if you considered your obedience to God a sacrifice?"

Pondering that question has helped me to develop a better understanding of what a "living sacrifice" really is: It's not a dead animal on an altar. It's a believer who has been made alive through Christ and who worshipfully offers his or her new life to God. When we sacrifice our entire lives to God, we're responding to God's mercy on our behalf through Christ.

In our day-to-day lives, we have opportunities to sacrifice our time, our resources and finances, and our comfort for the sake of God and others. We make sacrifices when we say no to our worldly desires (see Rom. 12:2); extend grace, mercy, and hospitality (see vv. 9–13); share in one another's burdens (see vv. 15–16); and offer forgiveness (see Eph. 4:32). Our loving obedience to God's commands may be costly and difficult for us, but it honors and strengthens our relationship with him (see Heb. 13:16). As Paul says in Romans 12, this *is* worship.

To be candid, I don't like the idea of being a "living sacrifice," because it feels so very costly. My natural tendency is to guard my time, my stuff, my comfort, my rights, my self. To make a sacrifice is to give up some or all of these things, and I find myself forced to wrestle with some uncomfortable questions: If I give this up today, do I trust that God will provide enough for tomorrow (see Luke 11:3)? Will I admit that my disobedience offends God and creates a breach in our relationship but that my obedience honors him and strengthens that relationship (see John 14:15–24)? Do I really believe that everything I have and everything I am (including my own body) comes from God and is not mine to hold on to in the first place (see 1 Chron. 29:14; Acts 17:28; 1 Cor. 6:19–20)? Have I actually taken to heart the sacrifice that Christ made on my behalf, when he shed his own blood to pay the price for my sins so that I could be forgiven (see Heb. 9:11–22; 12:1–4)?

Jesus sacrificed everything that was rightfully his to make me his own (see Heb. 10:1–18). Who am I to be stingy with my sacrifices? When faithful obedience feels costly, we can look to the sacrifice of Christ and the abundant provision of God and be strengthened to confidently bear that cost, knowing that our sacrifice will eventually bear fruit in our relationship with God and others.

Reflect: What does the word *sacrifice* mean to you? What has it meant to you when another person has made a sacrifice on your behalf?

Reflect: Look at the questions listed above. Which of them is most challenging or convicting to you? Why do you think that might be?

Act: Look for an opportunity today—even a small one—to sacrifice your time, resources, or comfort for the sake of someone else. Notice and pray about whatever might keep you from doing this.

ENDURING FOR THE LONG HAUL

Your season of singleness may last years, decades, or a lifetime. Honoring the Lord in our singleness and embracing this time of "undivided devotion" to him requires endurance. To run this race, we need God's strength, the nourishment of his Word, the encouragement of fellow believers, and a clear sight of the goal toward which we're running. It can be tempting to give up on our pursuit of ordinary faithfulness, but Scripture cheers us on (see Rom. 5:2–4; Col. 1:9–13; Heb. 12:1–17). In these last few days, we'll be reminded of why and how we can keep going.

DAY 28

A Beacon of Hope

*"You are the light of the world. A city set on a hill cannot be hidden. . . .
Let your light shine before others, so that they may see your good works
and give glory to your Father who is in heaven." (Matt. 5:14, 16)*

THE DAY-TO-DAY LABORS of following Christ in our singleness can become mundane and even burdensome, can't they? It is
especially then that we tend to forget that the way we live matters.
But whether we're conscious of it or not, people are paying attention, looking to our "manner of life" (Phil. 1:27) to learn something about what we believe, who God is, and whether or not his
Son really makes a difference in our lives. What will they see?

Through faithful obedience and humble repentance, we
honor God's place in our lives as King, worship him as Lord, and
reflect his heart of love and justice to those around us. Through
faithful presence and active involvement in our churches, we have
the opportunity to remind our brothers and sisters of our primary
identity as sons and daughters of God, cultivate growth in our
spiritual family, and testify to our Father's providence in the ups
and downs of this season. And through faithful endurance, our
actions, attitudes, and way of life can be a winsome representa-
tion of Jesus to a world that desperately longs for him.

In Matthew 5, Jesus tells his followers that they are the light
of the world. In a world full of darkness and confusion, people are
searching for light and often settling for darkness rather than the
light that Jesus offers. Our culture prizes dating and hooking up,
celebrates marriage as a right, and fears aloneness. And so living
a life of faithful singleness offers Christ's light and a surprising
countercultural message. In every aspect of life, we're more "anxious about the things of the Lord" (1 Cor. 7:32) than about the

world's darker alternatives. Even in the most mundane moments, the way we conduct ourselves is an opportunity to shine a light that reflects our Father.

What might the "good works" mentioned in today's verses look like for us in singleness? They may look like cultivating relationships that offer mutual encouragement and care and sacrificially loving those God has placed in our lives (see the friendship of Ruth and Naomi in the book of Ruth). We may serve in ways that strengthen and encourage the body of Christ, freely giving of our time, our resources, and ourselves (see 1 Cor. 12). We may embrace God's design for sexual faithfulness (see 1 Cor. 6:12–20) and seek the comfort of Christ in our sufferings rather than the many cheap comforts the world offers (see John 14:27; 2 Cor. 1:3–7). We may honor those we date or interact with as fellow image bearers and treat them with kindness and respect (see Rom. 12:10). We may trust God's provision in the face of fearful or worrisome things (see Phil. 4:4–7).

Of course, even as we do these good works, it is not our efforts or our successes that shine—it is Jesus, the "true light" (John 1:9). It is only through walking closely with him that we are strengthened and empowered to live faithful lives that might draw the eyes of others toward him.

Reflect: What aspects of faithful singleness seem most countercultural to you and to those with whom you interact? How could Jesus shine through your faithfulness in these areas?

Reflect: How could faithful singleness be a blessing and an example to our churches?

Act: Spend some time thinking about how you'd respond to someone who asked you why you live out your singleness in the way you do. If you have friends who've already asked questions along these lines, engage them in further conversation.

DAY 29

Scarcity or Sufficiency?

And my God will supply every need of yours according
to his riches in glory in Christ Jesus. (Phil. 4:19)

WHEN YOU THINK of a "scarcity mindset," perhaps you think of grandparents who lived through the Great Depression and tend to save and scrimp to ensure that there will always be enough. Or maybe you're the one still hoarding a stockpile of toilet paper, just in case we face another shortage like we did in 2020.

But a scarcity mindset can inform and motivate our approach to more than just stuff. A scarcity mindset can lead us to overwork and compete to get ahead, for fear of what will happen if we don't get that promotion or, worse, lose a job. It can lead us toward despair or compromise in the face of limited prospects for marriage and to view others as threats or competitors rather than fellow image bearers. Whether or not we're aware of it, this mindset is rooted in our view of God: Do we view him as a cold and distant miser who begrudgingly offers us only the bare minimum? Or do we view him as a generous Father who provides wisely for his children (see Matt. 7:7–11)?

Many of us have unfulfilled longings in our singleness that can easily tempt us to believe that God is withholding good gifts from us—we view him as a Scrooge rather than a benevolent Father. But over and over, Scripture tells us of God's provision, sufficiency, and even abundance (see Eph. 3:20–21). And on top of that, in today's verse Paul reminds us that God is rich! This world and everything in it belong to him, and anything we have is a gift from him (see Acts 17:25; James 1:17).

Paul wrote as one who had known scarcity but endured through it by God's strength (see Phil. 4:11–13). He wrote to a church that had given sacrificially on his behalf, assuring God's people that, as God had provided for him, God would provide for them as well. Just as Paul testified to and proclaimed God's sufficiency, we can remind ourselves of God's true nature and character, look back at his constant provision in our lives, and shift from a fearful scarcity mindset to one that rests in God's sufficiency.

Whatever God asks you to do, he will supply all you need. When he commands obedience, he will help you to be faithful. When he prompts you to give, you can give generously, knowing that you're merely sharing his gifts. When he gives someone else something you wish you had, he is still supplying every need of yours—even if his wise view of your needs is different from your own limited view. When you find yourself focusing on what you lack or fearing that there won't be enough, look to Christ. Paul could be confident of God's provision because he'd been assured that "in any and every circumstance" (Phil. 4:12) Christ strengthened him (see v. 13), and Christ will strengthen us as well. Through Christ, God has generously supplied all that we need to serve and honor him.

Reflect: In what areas do you find yourself operating out of a mindset of scarcity or a fear that there won't be "enough"?

Reflect: Do you tend to view and approach God as one who is stingy or generous? What do you think has led you to view him in this way?

Act: Take an opportunity this week to risk giving generously in some way. If you find yourself fearful or hesitant, pray about it and ask God to help you to give as a reflection of his own generous heart.

DAY 30

Look to Jesus

Therefore, since we are surrounded by so great a cloud of witnesses, let us also lay aside every weight, and sin which clings so closely, and let us run with endurance the race that is set before us, looking to Jesus, the founder and perfecter of our faith, who for the joy that was set before him endured the cross, despising the shame, and is seated at the right hand of the throne of God. (Heb. 12:1–2)

A LIFE OF faithfulness is much more like a marathon than a sprint, and those miles in the middle can feel especially long and hard. The author of Hebrews must have sensed this kind of weariness in his readers. Like a coach giving a pep talk to keep the team going, the writer looks back at those who've run before and looks to the One who has finished the race once and for all.

The "cloud of witnesses" described in Hebrews 11 is like a family history lesson, reminding contemporary believers of the faithful examples set by their forerunners in the faith. These are men and women who knew the cost of following God but who also saw him prove faithful time and time again. They waited, they longed for home, they sacrificed and suffered in their obedience to God. Abraham and Sarah spent much of their lives longing for children (see vv. 8–12). Rahab is remembered both for her checkered sexual past and the risk she took for a God who was not yet her own (see v. 31). We are in good company.

For these men and women, the Messiah was a distant hope. Now, surrounded by them, we can look together at Jesus, the fulfillment of that hope. The "founder and perfecter of our faith" lived his life on earth as a single man. He was a man of sorrows, acquainted with grief. He knew loneliness and rejection. He faced temptation, had brotherly friendships with women, and remained chaste. He sacrificed, suffered, and died for us. He has spent each and every day since then waiting for his betrothed. This Jesus knows our suffering, our weakness, our waiting and can truly say, "I get it."

Not only is Jesus uniquely able to sympathize with our weaknesses (see Heb. 4:15), he is also uniquely able to offer us comfort because of his own sufferings (see 2 Cor. 1:3–7). That comfort can strengthen us to endure, even when the race is long, painful, and exhausting. Whether we are struggling with aspects of faithful obedience that are unique to singleness or common to the Christian life, we can look to Jesus and all that he endured for our sake. When our faith itself feels weak, we can remember that completing this race depends not on the strength of our faith but on Jesus, the founder and perfecter of it. And along with him, we can look to the joy that awaits us at the finish line: rest in his presence and the final fulfillment of our longing for home (see Matt. 25:23; Heb. 6:10–12).

Reflect: What are some burdens or sins that make it hard for you to run the race of the Christian life with endurance?

Reflect: What aspects of Jesus's character and experience of life on earth are particularly meaningful and helpful to you as you endure right now?

Act: Write down these verses from Hebrews, or a few other verses that encourage you to look to Jesus for your endurance, and put them up where you'll see them often.

DAY 31

We're All Waiting for a Wedding

"Hallelujah! For the Lord our God the Almighty reigns. Let us rejoice and exult and give him the glory, for the marriage of the Lamb has come." (Rev. 19:6–7)

SOME LITTLE GIRLS and boys start dreaming of their weddings at a young age. No matter how much (or how little) any man or woman spends envisioning his or her wedding day, no one has spent as much time as God has spent preparing for the wedding feast of Christ and his bride, the church.

In Revelation 19, John records his vision of the marriage supper of the Lamb (see vv. 6–9; also 21:2, 9). This wedding is the consummation of a promise that's woven throughout Scripture: the Lord and his people will one day be united once and for all as a groom and his bride (see Isa. 54:5–6; Eph. 5:32). Anticipation heightened when John the Baptist took on the role of best man—rejoicing to make way for Jesus, the sacrificial "Lamb of God" (John 1:29). The bridegroom had come for his bride at last (see John 3:28–29), and he loved her so much that he bled and died to make her his own (see Eph. 5:25). In John's vision, the bride is adorned in wedding garments secured for her through that sacrifice (see Rev. 7:14; 19:8; see also Isa. 61:10).

Now Jesus is waiting for that wedding day. As he shared the cup with his disciples at the Last Supper, he told them, "I will not drink again of this fruit of the vine until that day when I drink it new with you in my Father's kingdom" (Matt. 26:29). On that day, the marriage of the Lamb to his bride will be cause for great rejoicing, as it will signal the completion of Christ's redemptive work and usher in the new heaven and new earth. We'll be with God, he will wipe away our tears and put an end to death and mourning, and all will be made new (see Rev. 21:1–5). Are you longing for that day to come too?

Even the most happily married people will tell you that earthly marriage isn't an arrival. It's not the end of problems or the beginning of bliss. It's just another season with unique blessings and challenges, one that still holds loneliness, disappointment, and grief. Marriage is not the end of waiting. In fact, earthly marriages will end when death parts husband and wife (see Matt. 22:30). Ultimately, we are *all* waiting for that final, glorious marriage of Christ and his church.

At a wedding, do you focus on the bride as she walks down the aisle, or do you watch the groom's face? I love imagining what Jesus's face might look like when he finally sees his bride. This future vision gives us hope and the promise that there's healing, restoration, and new life to come. Until that day, whether or not earthly marriage will be part of our story, we can devote ourselves to faithful love for Jesus's bride, the church, and to growing in love and knowledge of the bridegroom himself, Jesus.

Reflect: Read Ephesians 5:25–32, focusing on what it says about how Jesus loves his bride. What has he done for her? Why?

Reflect: How does it encourage you to know that all of us—even Jesus—are waiting together for the wedding feast of the Lamb?

Act: Whether or not you daydream about your own wedding, take some time—perhaps with a few friends—to imagine what the wedding feast of the Lamb and the new creation might look like. Let this stir up hope and encourage your heart in the midst of your own waiting.

Conclusion

As I was writing this devotional, a friend of mine, who as a third-grader is a little younger than my "target audience," assured me that she'd save up her money to buy her very own copy. She asked, "Will it help me to know the Bible better? I want to know the Bible better!"

I hope that when she reaches this conclusion, she'll say it has helped. My experience of singleness has certainly helped me to know my Bible better. Even when following Jesus in my singleness has been especially hard, I've still found Peter's words to Jesus resonating deep in my heart: "Lord, to whom shall we go? You have the words of eternal life" (John 6:68). Indeed, my life has depended on Jesus and the words of life offered on the pages of my Bible and repeated in the Holy Spirit's whispers (see John 14:26; Rom. 8:16).

God's Word consistently shows me his heart and character, teaches me who I am as his child, gives me permission and language to lament, invites me into relationship with the body of Christ, and calls me to abide with Jesus in both joy and suffering. Through Scripture I am reminded, again and again, that my hope is not in my circumstances, not in a husband or children or a tight circle of friends, not in my success or accomplishments, but in the steadfast love of Christ (see Ps. 146; Lam. 3:21–24; Heb. 6:19).

The Bible also reveals my idolatry, convicts me of my sin, and calls me to repentance. Through Scripture, I can know the One who sacrificially paid the price for my sin, who offers forgiveness and repairs the breach between me and God that my sin created (see 2 Cor. 5:16–21). Knowing the Bible has enabled me to know grace, comfort, and security that go far beyond what this world could ever offer.

Knowing Scripture has prepared me to expect and endure trouble, grief, and suffering in this life, but it has also assured me that my suffering will not be wasted (see Joel 2:25–27; 2 Cor. 1:3–7). The stories of Scripture and the example of Jesus show me what faithful, sacrificial love looks like. The Bible's many "one anothers" tell me that community is both essential and effortful and that it's part of what we're made for (see John 13:34–35; Rom. 12:10; 15:7, 14; Eph. 4:2, 32). It is not good, and I'd go as far as to say *not possible*, to faithfully live the Christian life alone (see Heb. 10:19–25). Even learning and living in obedience to God's Word is not just an individual endeavor but something we do together.

Through reading and remembering Scripture, studying it together with others, and feasting on it through corporate worship and preaching each Sunday, along with the Holy Spirit's work of bringing God's Word to mind when it's most needed, we are sustained. This is our spiritual daily bread. This is how we endure, how we grow toward maturity, how we continue to follow Jesus step-by-step. As we sink our roots down deep into the love of God (see Eph. 3:14–19), our lives will bear fruit and be a blessing to others (see John 15:1–10).

As you come to the end of these thirty-one readings, my prayer is that days 32, 33, and beyond will find you delving deeper into the Word of God, leaning a little harder on your community, and clinging more tightly to Christ. Some days that will be really hard to do. Some days the loneliness, the bitterness, or the fear will feel overwhelming. Some days it will feel like your community has failed you. Some days it might feel like God has failed you. But keep going. Keep following after the One who offers the words of life.

On those hard days, I pray you'll take comfort in the psalms of lament, finding words to voice your emotions, doubts, and complaints and gaining strength from the reminder that our God is big and loving enough to handle them all. I pray you'll draw closer to Jesus, who is well acquainted with hard days, even the darkest kind. I pray you'll have courage to take the risk of being vulnerable with your community, of letting people know when you're hurting or in need. And I pray that when you feel most vulnerable, most exposed, most alone, you will remember that God has you tucked safely under his wing and that you are clothed in Christ (see Ps. 91:1–4; Gal. 3:27).

If you are a pastor, ministry leader, counselor, or friend who loves and ministers to single people, I pray God's Word will nourish, equip, and comfort you as well. I hope that the things you've read in this devotional have encouraged you personally and not only as they pertain to your ministry to singles. I pray that God will give you compassion and tenderness for those who are single and the sensitivity and insight to know just how hard the hard days can be (may I suggest being prepared to offer a seat at your table, a good beverage, and a listening ear?). At the same time, I pray that if you're married, the single brothers and sisters in your life will be a source of encouragement to you and that they'll point you to Jesus through their pursuit of faithfulness.

We're on this road together. I eagerly await the day when we all arrive and take our seats at the great wedding feast that God is preparing for us even now. That will indeed be a very good day.

Acknowledgments

To the likes of the late Dr. Jim Farrell, Benjamin Smith, and Christy Risher Campbell, for seeing a writer in me.

To my friends at YouthWorks, who entrusted an eager twentysomething with so many huge responsibilities that shaped who I am, how I do ministry, how I live my singleness, and how I write devotionals. Mad props to Potts, Mara, Sam, Ben, Kari, Kate, and Nachelle.

To Abby and Julie, without whose moral support this book would never have happened.

To Jessica, Linda, David, Stephanie, Rick, Sue, Jen, Jason, and others who shared their insights and feedback and asked good questions along the way.

To Deepak, Amanda, and the editorial team at P&R, for making this an infinitely better, richer, more gospel-saturated book than it would have been otherwise.

To my family, for your support and care and for sharing me first with Birmingham and now with St. Louis.

To my professors at Covenant Theological Seminary, for teaching me as well as showing me how to love and steward God's Word in order to love and serve his people.

To Rev. Andrew Vander Maas, who first posed the question that has shaped years of my singleness. Thank you for your influence in the creation of a church culture that loves and includes single people.

To Rev. Daniel Song, the truest of brothers. Thank you for believing in me, preaching the gospel to me, and taking care of the mice.

To the elders of Crossroads and Restoration, who have loved me, valued me, made space for me, and freed me to write. Thank you for being faithful shepherds. Mike Going, I'm looking at you, sir, since you insisted on being named.

To the families who have claimed me and always keep a seat open at their table for me, I love you. Thank you for being a constant reminder that I am not alone.

To the friends who've prayed me through this. I don't take for granted that y'all are too many to name here.

Lastly, to my Restoration family, thank you for being the church to me and to one another. It is a joy to serve you and an abundant gift to be loved by you.

Jesus, I'm yours, and so is this book. Thank you for being Immanuel.

Notes

Day 5: Your Body Matters

1. Jesus is hungry in Matthew 21:18, needs sleep in Luke 8:23, is touched in Mark 5:30–31, suffers physically due to emotional distress in Luke 22:44, endures pain throughout the crucifixion accounts in all four gospels, and is described as being tempted "in every way" (Heb. 4:15 NIV).

2. If you would like to learn more about the significance of our union with Christ, I highly recommend Rankin Wilbourne's book *Union with Christ: The Way to Know and Enjoy God* (Colorado Springs: David C. Cook, 2016).

Day 7: Belonging to the Body

1. Examples of other descriptions of the church include a family/household (see Gal. 6:10; Eph. 2:19), a building (see Eph. 2:19–22; 1 Peter 2:5), and the bride of Christ (see Eph. 5:31–32; Rev. 21:9). We'll look at that last one further on day 31.

Day 8: Tending to Friendships

1. Wesley Hill's book *Spiritual Friendship: Finding Love in the Church as a Celibate Gay Christian* (Grand Rapids: Brazos Press, 2015) explores both our current cultural moment and the history of friendship in the church.

Day 12: An Invitation to Lament

1. I am indebted to the late Dr. David Calhoun, whose class on sickness and suffering at Covenant Theological Seminary in the spring of 2010 introduced me to a robust understanding of lament. His commendation of Michael Card's book *A Sacred Sorrow: Reaching Out to God in the Lost Language of Lament* (Colorado Springs: NavPress, 2005) helped to deepen my appreciation of lament.

Day 13: Mourning What's Lost

1. Kelly Haer, "RelateStrong: Singleness," chap. 2 in *Vital Tools for Relevant Church Leaders: Restoring Relationships and Building*

Community During Difficult Conversations (Malibu, CA: Boone Center for the Family, 2019), https://family.pepperdine.edu /relatestrong-leadership-series/ebook-download.htm.

Day 16: Empty Womb and Empty Arms

1. "Prophetic Paradox," chapter 3 of Barry Danylak's book *Redeeming Singleness: How the Storyline of Scripture Affirms the Single Life* (Wheaton, IL: Crossway, 2010) looks at the eunuch, barren woman, and spiritual offspring in depth.

Day 19: Fear and Anxiety

1. If this is true for you, I'd encourage you to talk with your doctor or a mental health professional, along with a pastor or ministry leader.

Day 20: Preaching to Our Self-Pity

1. *Merriam-Webster*, s.v. "self-pity (*n.*)," accessed September 26, 2020, https://www.merriam-webster.com/dictionary/self-pity.

Day 23: Discernment in Dating

1. Both Scripture and common wisdom suggest that it is a sin for a born-again Christian to marry a non-Christian. First Corinthians 7:12–16 is addressed to those who became believers after marriage, and Paul presumes that there could be difficulty or discord in their marriages. He is not commending getting married for the sake of converting someone. Paul later in the same chapter tells Christian widows that they should marry "only in the Lord" (v. 39). Thus, Paul says a Christian *must* marry another Christian. Kathy Keller addresses the topic of whether Christians should marry non-Christians in a helpful and concise article ("Don't Take It from Me: Reasons You Should Not Marry an Unbeliever," The Gospel Coalition, January 22, 2012, https:// www.thegospelcoalition.org/article/dont-take-it-from-me -reasons-you-should-not-marry-an-unbeliever). If finding a spouse is one of the main goals of dating (and I'd suggest it is), it is best to date someone who is already a Christian.

2. The NIV translation of Proverbs 4:23 reads, "Above all else, guard your heart." In context, however, this verse is talking about guarding against sin rather than protecting against relational vulnerability.

Day 24: Sexual Faithfulness

1. This is especially true for those of us who grew up in the church in the 1980s and 1990s. I'm encouraged that many youth groups and college ministries are beginning to disciple students with a more holistic view of biblical sexuality. Beth Felker Jones's book *Faithful: A Theology of Sex* (Grand Rapids: Zondervan, 2015) is a very helpful contribution to that effort.

2. *Sexual faithfulness* is a term I am using to encompass the pursuit of fidelity to a biblical sexual ethic, including but not limited to celibacy outside marriage.

3. The list of suggested resources on page 97 includes a number of books that address this topic. Jones's *Faithful* is a great starting point.

Day 26: Honoring Marriages

1. If a friend is struggling with sexual issues in his or her marriage, encourage this person to seek out the guidance of a counselor, ministry leader, or medical professional (depending on the nature of the issues). Additional resources may be available through Harvest USA at www.harvestusa.org or similar ministries in your area.

Suggested Resources
for the Journey

Allberry, Sam. *7 Myths about Singleness*. Wheaton, IL: Cross-way, 2019. [This book addresses many practical aspects of singleness and invites single people to see the opportunities afforded to them. It is also a great conversation starter for churches that want to think about how to care for and encourage single people.]

Danylak, Barry. *Redeeming Singleness: How the Storyline of Scripture Affirms the Single Life*. Wheaton, IL: Crossway, 2010. [This is the most academic book on the list but is the best treatment I've seen of a robust theology of singleness drawn from the entirety of the biblical storyline.]

Harrison, Glynn. *A Better Story: God, Sex, and Human Flourishing*. London: Inter-Varsity Press, 2016. [This resource gives a more in-depth look at how we can engage our culture's current views of sexuality with a biblical response.]

Hill, Wesley. *Spiritual Friendship: Finding Love in the Church as a Celibate Gay Christian*. Grand Rapids: Brazos Press, 2015. [Hill explores the need we all—married and single—have for friendship and helps us to think about how churches can be inclusive of single adults. Although not without controversy, Hill's insights are valuable additions to conversations on singleness and the church. You can also read my review: "Spiritual Friendship by Wesley Hill," Allkirk Network, August 10, 2015, https://allkirk.net/2015/08/10/review -spiritual-friendship-by-wesley-hill/.]

Jones, Beth Felker. *Faithful: A Theology of Sex*. Grand Rapids: Zondervan, 2015. [A brief but rich theology of sex that is written at a level accessible for high school and college students. It is remarkably inclusive of single people and casts a vision of biblical sexuality that is solid and compelling.]

Winner, Lauren F. *Real Sex: The Naked Truth about Chastity.* Grand Rapids: Brazos Press, 2005. [Though this book is several years old now, it continues to be helpful for presenting a robust picture of how faithful singleness can be lived out in the context of the local church.]

BIBLICAL
COUNSELING
COALITION

The Biblical Counseling Coalition (BCC) is passionate about enhancing and advancing biblical counseling globally. We accomplish this through broadcasting, connecting, and collaborating.

Broadcasting promotes gospel-centered biblical counseling ministries and resources to bring hope and healing to hurting people around the world. We promote biblical counseling in a number of ways: through our *15:14* podcast, website (biblicalcounselingcoalition.org), partner ministry, conference attendance, and personal relationships.

Connecting biblical counselors and biblical counseling ministries is a central component of the BCC. The BCC was founded by leaders in the biblical counseling movement who saw the need for and the power behind building a strong global network of biblical counselors. We introduce individuals and ministries to one another to establish gospel-centered relationships.

Collaboration is the natural outgrowth of our connecting efforts. We truly believe that biblical counselors and ministries can accomplish more by working together. The BCC Confessional Statement, which is a clear and comprehensive definition of biblical counseling, was created through the cooperative effort of over thirty leading biblical counselors. The BCC has also published a three-part series of multi-contributor works that bring theological wisdom and practical expertise to pastors, church leaders, counseling practitioners, and students. Each year we are able to facilitate the production of numerous resources, including books, articles, videos, audio resources, and a host of other helps for biblical counselors. Working together allows us to provide robust resources and develop best practices in biblical counseling so that we can hone the ministry of soul care in the church.

To learn more about the BCC, visit biblicalcounselingcoalition.org.

Living Faithfully—Heart First

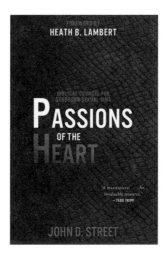

Honest self-assessment is hard. Even Christians trust their hearts more than they should. And when the heart is filled with rage ("I will have my own way"), sensuality ("I will gratify myself regardless of the sin involved"), or pride ("I deserve whatever my heart desires"), indulging its desires all too easily leads to acts that were previously unimaginable.

This book is an excellent resource for all who want to understand how the passions and motivations of their hearts can lead them into sins of any kind. Using this resource, readers can learn to identify and resist sinful passions. By the grace of God, the worst sins can be forgiven in Christ.

"The unfolding of the truth about the heart is for any malady of the soul. This book can instruct the reader to develop good devotional and Bible-reading habits to overcome the temptations of sin in all areas of life. This book contains so many jewels for understanding the heart that reading it [is] like searching for gold."
   —**Bill Shannon**, Pastor of Discipleship Counseling, Grace Community Church, Sun Valley, California

"The survey of diagnostic questions is itself worth the price of the book."
   —**Stuart W. Scott**, Professor of Biblical Counseling, The Master's University

Did you find this book helpful?
Consider leaving a review online.
The author appreciates your feedback!

Or write to P&R at editorial@prpbooks.com
with your comments. We'd love to hear from you.